*The* ***USS ENGLAND DE635,*** *was a typical Buckley Class Destroyer Escort. Shown here in February 1944, with dark camouflage paint and the letters "DE" before her hull number. This was done so identification between escorts and destroyers could be distinguished between each other. The* ***USS ENGLAND*** *would go on to sink six Japanese submarines in the Pacific in only twelve days, in May 1944.* 19N60938

# DESTROYER ESCORTS OF WORLD WAR TWO

by Thomas F. Walkowiak

## INTRODUCTION

The development of the Destroyer Escort as known in World War Two apparently started in June 1939. Commander R.B. Carney, United States Navy, suggested a design for an intermediate second line torpedo craft. The hope was that this craft could be mass produced in case of war. He felt that the design of the ships then being built could not be mass produced quickly enough. By September, the War Plans Division of the Bureau of Ships suggested that a design be drawn up for an escort vessel.

Several different design studies were made and cancelled for various reasons. Then in January 1941, Admiral Stark, then Commander in Chief of the US Fleet, asked for recommendations on types of small craft to be procured for late 1941. The recommendation was for 50 escort vessels for convoy protection. In February 1941, the Secretary of the Navy, authorized the construction of the 50 vessels when design studies were completed. However, the General Board (1) was unhappy with the design studies submitted and on 19 May 1941, these ships were cancelled. In March 1941, the lend-lease law was written into law.

Act of 11 March 1941: "...Notwithstanding the provisions of any other law, the President may, from time to time, when he deems it in the interest of national defense, authorize...the Secretary of the Navy, or the head of any other department or agency of the government:" (1) To manufacture in arsenals, factories and shipyards under their jurisdiction or otherwise procure, to the extent to which funds are made available therefore, or contracts are authorized from time to time by Congress, or both, any defense the President deems vital to the defense of the United States.
"(2) To sell, transfer title to, exchange, lease, lend or otherwise dispose of, to any such Government any defense article,... The value of defense article disposed of...shall not exceed $1,300,000,000...."

1. The General Board was a group of senior naval officers from different bureaus that determined the mission requirements of each type of ship and the characteristics of the ships to carry out their mission.

Thus Lend-Lease was started and along with it, the lending of 50 US Navy Four Stack Destroyers to the Royal Navy. In mid June 1941, the British, with desperate need for more escorts, requested that the US Navy build 50 new escorts for the Royal Navy. President Roosevelt approved the production of these 50 British DE's (BDE) on 15 August 1941. The first of these new vessels was laid down at Mare Island Navy Yard in Vallejo, California on February 28, 1942. This was the **USS BRENNAN DE13** (ex BDE BENTINCK).

The design concepts were to meet British requirements. However, many changes were made in the design due to shortages in weapons and powerplants. After the entry of the United States into the war, the need for escorts for the US Navy became apparent. Some of the vessels being built for the Royal Navy were kept for the US Navy. Also, many more Destroyer Escorts were ordered. Of the 1,005 escorts ordered during the course of the war, only 563 were built. The rest were cancelled during the war, and of the completed Destroyer Escorts, 78 were delivered to England. A few were also given to France during the war.

Due to the armament and powerplant configurations, the Destroyer Escorts of WW2 were broken down into six classes. These were the "Short Hull" **EVARTS** class (3" gunned, GMT-GM Tandem Diesel), **BUCKLEY** class (3" gunned, TE-Turbo-Electric), **CANNON** class (3" gunned, DET-Diesel-Electric-Tandem type), **EDSALL** class (3" gunned, FMR-Fairbanks-Morris Reduction gear type), **RUDDERROW** class (5" gunned, TEV-Turbo-Electric drive) and the **JOHN C. BUTLER** class (5" gunned, WGT-Westinghouse Geared Turbine). Also, the conversion of 95 "TE" and "TEV" to APD's (High Speed Transports).

The last active World War Two Destroyer Escort to serve with the US Navy was the **USS PARLE DE708.** She served as a NRF ship into 1970.

***USS BRENNAN DE 13**, was the first Destroyer Escort for use by the US Navy. This censored photograph, which on the radar screens was omitted, was taken in March 1943. The aft 1.1" machine gun is also censored.* *80G40920*

# ORDNANCE

**3"/50 Cal Mk22 Gun** This single open mount was developed in the late 1930's and was used onboard the "GMT, TE, FMR and DET" classes of Destroyer Escorts. This weapon had very limited firepower, but was lightweight and easy to operate. It fired a fixed round which was hand loaded and was the smallest gun that could fire the newly developed VT-Fused projectile.

**5"/38 Cal Mk30 Gun** This single enclosed mount was the Main Battery onboard the "WGT and TEV" classes of Destroyer Escorts. Also it was installed on the 3" gunned ships that were converted to APD's. Developed in the 1930's, this dual-purpose weapon was a vast improvement over the 3". The 5" gun was the mainstay of the US Navy during the war and for many years after.

**1.1" Quad Mk1 Gun Mount** It was developed in the 1930's as an automatic anti-aircraft weapon. This quadruple, open gun started to appear in the fleet in numbers by 1940. This weapon proved to be very ineffective and was replaced by the 40mm gun. A number of 1.1" guns remained on Destroyer Escorts until the end of the war. However, all 1.1" guns were ordered scrapped by late 1945.

**40mm Twin Mk1 Gun Mount** It was developed in the early 1940's as a replacement for the 1.1" gun. This weapon proved to be a very popular gun and became the standard anti-aircraft guns of the US Navy during the war. It proved to be very effective and easy to operate.

**40mm Quad Mk2 Gun Mount** It was basically the same as the twin, but with two twin guns mounted on a single mount. It had a very high rate of fire with the projectile weight of over twice the 1.1" round. These power driven mounts were also director controlled.

**40mm Single Mk3 Gun** It was adopted from an Army gun in 1943 during the Battle of Anzio, to add more anti-aircraft protection. These guns were manually operated and pipe rail guards were needed to prevent the gun crews from firing into their own ship. When the guns were added to Destroyer Escorts, the Triple Torpedo Tubes were removed.

**20mm Oerlikon Gun** The standard small anti-aircraft gun of the US Navy during the war. Developed in the early 1940's from a Swiss design, this gun was first test fired in June 1941. By December 1941, over 350 guns were in use by the US Fleet. This weapon was a manually operated machine gun that fired a fixed round from a magazine. The most common type was the Mk4 single mount. The 20mm was a replacement for the ineffective .50 cal machine gun.

*An excellent forward view of the **USS GILMORE DE18** clearly shows her 3" guns and hedgehog launcher. Above number two 3" gun is mounted a single 20mm Gun, which is equipped with a MK14 gun sight. Also installed on the bridge is an MK52 gun director. A fresh coat of paint is being applied to the forecastle deck, in this March 1945 photograph.* *19N80082*

**Triple Torpedo Tube** All classes of Destroyer Escorts, except the EVARTS class were designed with the Triple Torpedo Tube. These fired the standard 21" Mk15 Surface Torpedo that carried an 825 pound TNT warhead. The mount was located on the superstructure deck amidships.

**Depth Charge Track** All classes of Destroyer Escorts carried a pair of Depth Charge Tracks on the stern. These tracks carried a number of the US Navy standard "ash can" type charge, which was filled with 300 pounds of TNT, or the faster sinking Mk9 "tear drop" Depth Charge.

**"K" Gun Projector** This device was used to project a Depth Charge, by means of a powder charge, away from the ship, which gave a better Depth Charge pattern for attacking a submarine. Each Destroyer Escort carried 8 projectors near the stern with 4 per side. A roller rack was located along side each "K" gun, which held several Depth Charges and made the gun easier to load.

**Hedgehog Launcher** This was an ahead-throwing weapon located on the Main Deck just aft of the first main battery gun. Developed by the British in the early 1940's, this "spigot-mortar" proved to be a very effective weapon against submarines. The Hedgehog fired a 24 round contact-fused submarine size pattern. Each round had a 30 pound TNT warhead.

*A close-up of the forward 5" gun on board the* ***USS TWEEDY DE532.*** *This shot was taken during the winter of 43/44 at Boston Navy Yard where she was built. The rear of the shields on the back of the 5" gun had a sloped back to give clearance for the firing of the hedgehog. In the rear is the* ***USS OSBERG DE538*** *which is still being built.* USN

*Still being fitted out, the* ***USS LEVY DE162,*** *has had her three "K" gun roller racks and depth charge tracks already installed. The stacked tanks mounted on the stern are the smoke screen generators. Yet to be installed is the aft anti-aircraft gun and director.* USN

# DIRECTORS & ELECTRONICS

**Mk51 Gun Director** This was an open pedestal mounted device used for the 1.1" and 40mm power driven guns. Mounted with a Mk14 lead-computing gun sight, this proved to be the standard Director of this type during the war.

**Mk52 Gun Director** It was developed from the Mk51 Director with the improved Mk15 Gun Sight and Mk26 Range-only Radar installed. This Director started to appear onboard Destroyer Escorts in late 1944 and became the standard main battery director on all Destroyer Escorts.

**"SL" Radar** It was a S-band surface search radar developed in the early 1940's. This was located in a 42" diameter protective dome on the foremast and had a range of approximately 13 miles.

**"SU Radar"** This was an improved version of the "SL" Radar. This had a range of about 18 miles. It was located on the foremast in place of the "SL" in a 24" diameter dome.

*A close-up of an unknown Destroyer Escort in 1945 with the recently installed MK52 gun director where the range finder was installed, which now has been moved forward of the MK52 director. During this yard period the installation of "Nancy" lights and other types of unknown lights along the bridge bulwark.* USN

*This electronic identification photograph taken of the* ***USS CONNOLLY DE306*** *in July 1944 shows radars and radio antennas. The Radio Direction Finder Loop is visible on the platform aft of the mast.* NH64655

**"SA Radar"** This was the "bed-spring" type radar screen located atop the foremast. It was an air-search radar with a range of about 12 miles. Built by RCA, the screen was 8'9" x 5' and was the primary air-search radar used by Destroyer Escorts during the war.

**"HF/DF"** It was a Radio Direction Finder type of antenna that was used to locate radio transmitting submarines. It was located atop of the foremast in place of the "SA" radar on some units. Later the "HF/DF" was moved to a stub mainmast located aft of the Torpedo Tubes.

**SONAR** The Destroyer Escorts of World War Two used the "QC" series of SONAR. This was enclosed in a retractable dome located at the bottom of the hull.

# DESTROYER ESCORT CAMOUFLAGE

## BY

## DAVID SHADELL

The paint schemes for the destroyer escort classes followed the standard practices followed by the warships of the two major fleets of the U.S. Navy. At the start of the DE building programs both fleets were painted in different measures but had a uniform appearance throughout each fleet. In the Atlantic Fleet all ships were painted measure 22, two tone concealment camouflage effective against submarine and surface observation. The Pacific Fleet painted their ships measure 21, overall navy Blue, a concealment camouflage effective against aerial observation.

The Navy's publication which controlled camouflage painting was referred to as "SHIPS 2" originally distributed to the fleet in 1937. The March, 1943, supplement to "SHIPS 2" introduced the dazzle, disruptive camouflage measures 31 dark pattern system, 32 medium pattern system, and 33 light pattern system. In the Pacific Fleet, these new measures were not adopted until October, 1943. However, the first DEs to wear a dazzle paint scheme were not painted until January, 1944, (DE-789-32/11d and DE-794-31/14d). Many DEs destined for the Pacific Fleet followed suit, there finally being 30 measure 31 and 32, 5-measure 33a and 4 other patterns drawn for DE use. Dazzle painting for the Pacific Fleet was discontinued officially on January 1, 1945, substituting measures 12, 21, and 22 for the measures 31, 32, and 33. Paint colors were also changed at this time from the purple blue tinted paints which had been used throughout the war to a series of neutral gray paints which corresponded to the old paints and nomenclature. Although the Pacific Fleet directive called for repainting as soon as possible, the accelerated pace of operations and the slow delivery of the new neutral gray paints caused some units to continue to wear their dazzle pattern camouflage paint schemes for some months. A few vessels were still wearing their pattern paint when hostilities against Japan ended in August, 1945.

In the Atlantic Fleet where measure 22 was still considered to be a very effective camouflage paint scheme, the first use of dazzle painted ships did not begin until the spring of 1944, using design 3d exclusively. Dazzle painting not being officially acknowledged until July, 1944, and again specifying the use of 3d patterns. Not until December, 1944, did CINCLANT sanction the use of measure 21, 32, and 33, for general use in the Atlantic Fleet. Some ships retained their measure 22 paint scheme throughout the war. As the Atlantic Fleet was now seriously out of step with the Pacific Fleet,

***DE-795* GUNASON** *photographed shortly after completion in February, 1944, wearing camouflage measure 13, all horizontal surfaces painted haze gray (5-H). By April, 1944, following her shakedown training, she had been repainted into camouflage measure 22. Buships had directed that new construction vessels be completed in the paint scheme of the fleet of its ultimate assignment. However, if this were not known at the time of completion, then the vessel would be painted measure 13, haze gray. Due to the vast number of vessels in the DE building program and the incredibly fast building times of some units, the use of this expedient paint scheme was more prevalent than in other classes of USN ships. Gunason's wartime duties included convoy escort missions to the Caribbean, Mediterranean, and England. Toward the end of January, 1945, she departed for the Pacific where she continued her escort duties principally among the Philippine Islands.* *19N62869*

**DE-152 PETERSON** *photographed off the New York Navy Yard on July 7, 1944, wearing camouflage measure 31/3d. At this time 3d was the only dazzle pattern authorized for use on Atlantic Fleet vessels. This particular 3d pattern was originally drawn for short-hulled DEs but was painted on long-hull DEs as well. As specified in the design drawing haze gray (5-H) was to be the lightest color in the design along with ocean gray (5-O) and dull black (BK). However, light gray (5-L) appears to have been substituted, thus changing the pattern designation from 31/3d to 32/3d. Peterson is an excellent example of an Atlantic Fleet Destroyer Escort showing 3d pattern, extra single army pattern 40mm gun mounts and HF/DF positioned on the mainmast. On April 16, 1944, Peterson along with Gandy (DE-764) and Joyce (DE-317) while escorting a convoy from New York to Northern Ireland combined to sink U-550.* *USN*

***APD-63 LLOYD** photographed on September 15, 1944, upon completion of her conversion from destroyer escort configuration to a fast transport at the Philadelphia Navy Yard. She is painted in camouflage measure 31/20L which was developed to blend the APD into the lush tropical background of the Philippines Islands. Design 20L employed the use of a master scheme over which was laid an outline of the ship to be painted. Many amphibious ships and crafts wore this concealment measure. Upon her arrival in the Western Pacific, she became Flagship of Transport Division 103. Lloyd participated in a number of invasions in the Philippines and Dutch East Indies. She was responsible for knocking out an enemy shore battery and splashing 4 enemy suicide aircraft.* USN

CINCLANT directed in March of 1945, the use of the same painting measures as the Pacific Fleet (measures 12, 21, and 22). Thus making both fleet's directives uniform. In the Atlantic Fleet the change to the new measures and paints was much more leisurely, as CINCLANT's directive specified repainting during the next regularly scheduled overhaul. Shortly after VJ day, CINCLANT respecified the use of measure 22 as the paint for all Atlantic Fleet ships.

The use of these standard paint schemes continued for some units at least into 1947, particularly measure 22. By the time of the Korean War, all vessels were painted overall #27, haze gray, which was war time measure 13 using the neutral gray paints and is still used as the Navy's service paint of today.

The APD conversions did not follow normal warship painting practices. They were painted in the measure 31 green patterns developed for amphibious vessels. Most of the APDs to wear measure 31 camouflage wore measure 31/20L which was developed in the summer of 1944, for the Philippines campaign. Design 20L used warm tropical green paints. In the spring of 1945, new measures and new paints were developed, specifying larger patterns and cooler hues of greens. However, these were painted on only a few units. Towards the end of the war most vessels were completed in measure 21 neutral Navy Gray.

# EVARTS CLASS

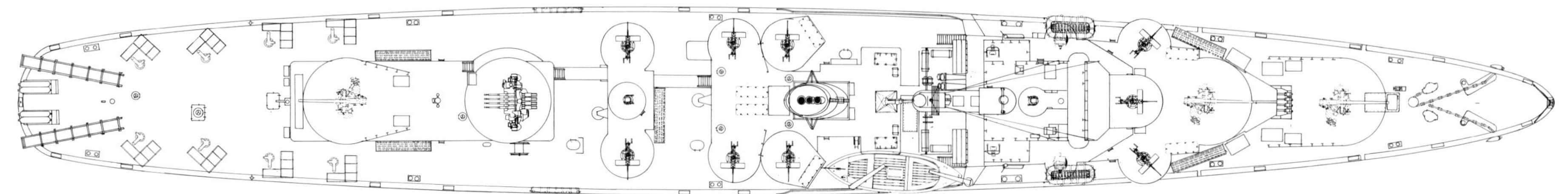

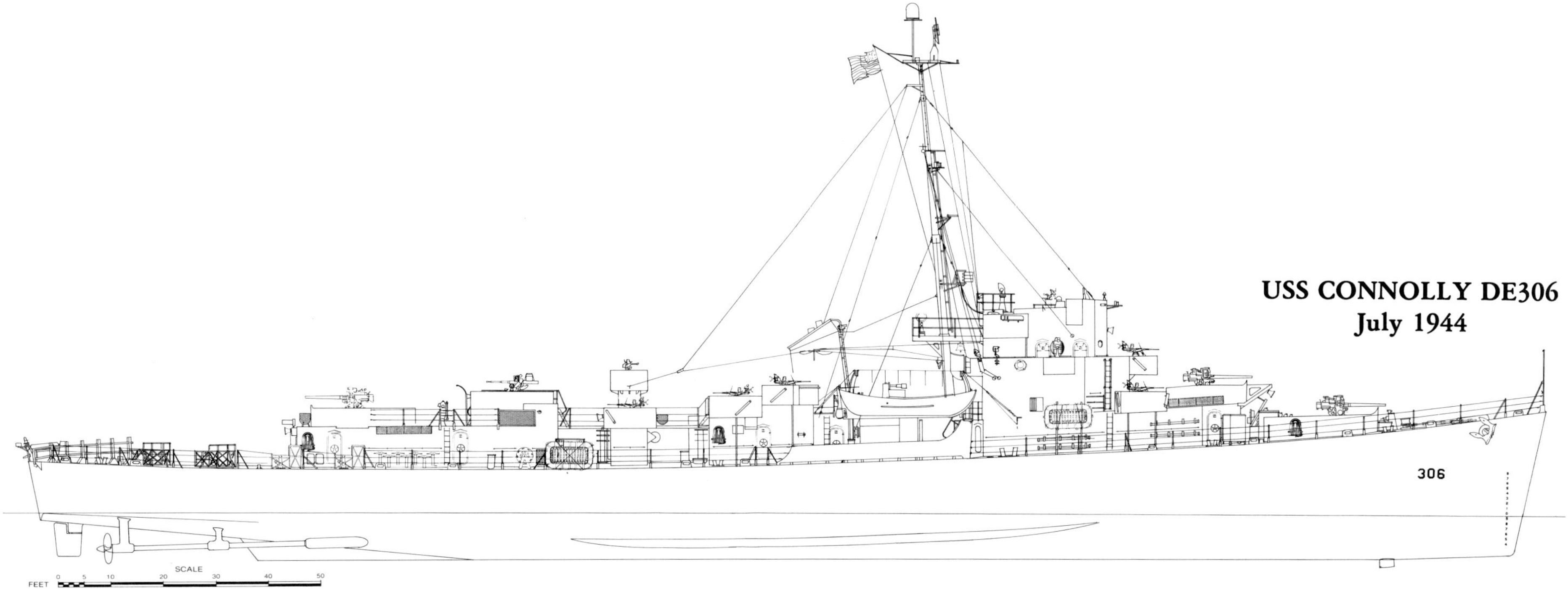

**USS CONNOLLY DE306**
**July 1944**

306

SCALE
FEET 0 5 10 20 30 40 50

*The* ***USS ENGSTROM DE50*** *just out of overhaul, is heading for the Pacific in the February 1945 photograph. She is carrying a typical late war fitout of "SA" radar, twin 40mm guns and MK14 equipped 20mm guns. Also, a MK52 director on the bridge. She is but one of the 65 EVARTS built for the US Navy during the war.* *19N79871*

## EVARTS Class

**DE5-50, 256-265, 301-307, 527-530**

### GENERAL INFORMATION

| | |
|---|---|
| Length Overall | 289'-5" |
| Length at Waterline 283'-6" | 283'-6" |
| Beam | 35'-1" |
| Shaft Horsepower | 6,000 |
| Trail Speed | 21.5 Knots |
| War Endurance | 4,150 Miles/12 Knots |
| Displacement | 1,436 Tons |
| Complement | 15 Officers 183 Men |
| Fuel Capacity | 198 Tons Diesel |

### ARMAMENT

3-3"/50 cal guns-Main Battery
1-Twin 40mm gun (DE13-18, 45) or 1.1" gun
(DE5-11, 19-44, 47-50, 256-265, 301-307, 527-530).
9-20mm Single guns
1-Hedgehog
2-Depth Charge Tracks
8-"K" gun projectors

This class was the first of the Destroyer Escorts to be built and the USS BRENNAN DE13 was the first. It was built by Mare Island Navy Ship Yard and launched on August 22, 1942, Lcdr H.A. Adams, Jr. was commanding. A total of 97 ships were built with 32 going to Great Britain before commissioning into the US Navy. Also known as the GMT (General Motors Tandem Diesel) or short hull Destroyer Escort. Proved to be unsuccessful, these ships were stricken and scrapped after the war. Two (DE6 and 47) were given to the Chinese Navy in August 1945.

*Wearing war paint, this May 1944 photograph shows the* **USS GRISWOLD DE7** *heading out from Mare Island Shipyard overhaul. She is still carrying the range finder on her bridge and 1.1" guns aft.* USN

BUILDING YARDS

| | |
|---|---|
| BethHI | Bethelehem Steel, Hingham, MA |
| BethQ | Bethlehem Quincy, MA |
| BethSF | Bethlehem San Francisco |
| BosNY | Boston Navy Yard |
| Brown | Brown Shipbuilding, Houston, TX |
| ChrNY | Charleston Navy Yard |
| Cons | Consolidated, Orange, TX |
| Defoe | Defoe, Bay City, MI |
| Dravo | Dravo, Pittsburgh, PA |
| Fedrl | Federal Shipbuilding, Newark, NJ |
| MINY | Mare Island Navy Yard |
| NorNY | Norfolk Navy Yard |
| PHNY | Philadelphia Navy Yard |
| PSNY | Puget Sound Navy Yard |
| TampSB | Tampa Shipbuilding, Tampa, FL |
| WPS | Western Pipe & Steel, San Pedro, CA |

ABBREVIATIONS

| | |
|---|---|
| APD | Fast Troop Transport |
| ASW | Anti-Submarine Warfare Ship |
| CG | US Coast Guard |
| DER | Destroyer Escort Radar Picket |
| IX | Miscellaneous Ship |
| NRF | Naval Reserve Force |

*These British Destroyer Escorts are still being built at Mare Island. Note the doors and hatches stowed on deck ready to be installed.* USN

## EVARTS (GMT) CLASS

| | | | | | |
|---|---|---|---|---|---|
| DE5 | EVARTS | BosNY | 15/ 4/43 | 2/10/45 | Scrapped 7/46 |
| DE6 | WYFFELS | " | 21/ 4/43 | 25/ 9/45 | China BU72 |
| DE7 | GRISWOLD | " | 28/ 4/43 | 19/11/45 | Scrapped 1/47 |
| DE8 | STEELE | " | 4/ 5/43 | 28/11/45 | Scrapped 1/47 |
| DE9 | CARLSON | " | 10/ 5/43 | 10/12/45 | Scrapped 12/46 |
| DE10 | BEBAS | " | 15/ 5/43 | 18/10/45 | Scrapped 2/47 |
| DE11 | CROUTERS | " | 25/ 5/43 | 30/11/45 | Scrapped 12/46 |
| DE13 | BRENNAN | MINY | 20/ 1/43 | 9/10/45 | Scrapped 8/46 |
| DE14 | DOHERTY | " | 6/ 2/43 | 14/12/45 | Scrapped 12/46 |
| DE15 | AUSTIN | " | 13/ 2/43 | 21/12/45 | Scrapped 2/47 |
| DE16 | E.G.CHASE | " | 20/ 3/43 | 16/10/45 | Scrapped 4/47 |
| DE17 | E.C.DALY | " | 3/ 4/43 | 20/12/45 | Scrapped 2/47 |
| DE18 | GILMORE | " | 17/ 4/43 | 29/12/45 | Scrapped 3/47 |
| DE19 | B.R.HASTINGS | " | 1/ 5/43 | 25/10/45 | Scrapped 3/47 |
| DE20 | LE HARDY | " | 15/ 5/43 | 25/10/45 | Scrapped 1/47 |
| DE21 | H.C.THOMAS | " | 31/ 5/43 | 26/10/45 | Scrapped 2/47 |
| DE22 | WILEMAN | " | 11/ 6/43 | 16/11/45 | Scrapped 2/47 |
| DE23 | C.R.GREER | " | 25/ 6/43 | 2/11/45 | Scrapped 3/47 |
| DE24 | WHITMAN | " | 3/ 7/43 | 16/11/45 | Scrapped 2/47 |
| DE25 | WINTLE | " | 10/ 7/43 | 14/11/45 | Scrapped 8/47 |
| DE26 | DEMPSEY | " | 24/ 7/43 | 22/11/45 | Scrapped 5/47 |
| DE27 | DUFFY | " | 5/ 8/43 | 9/11/45 | Scrapped 8/47 |
| DE28 | EMERY | " | 14/ 8/43 | 15/11/45 | Scrapped 8/47 |
| DE29 | STADFELD | " | 26/ 8/43 | 10/11/45 | Scrapped 8/47 |
| DE30 | MARTIN | " | 4/ 9/43 | 19/11/45 | Scrapped 7/47 |
| DE31 | SEDERSTROM | " | 11/ 9/43 | 15/11/45 | Scrapped 2/48 |
| DE32 | FLEMING | " | 18/ 9/43 | 10/11/45 | Scrapped 3/48 |
| DE33 | TISDALE | " | 11/10/43 | 12/10/45 | Scrapped 3/48 |
| DE34 | EISELE | " | 18/10/43 | 16/11/45 | Scrapped 2/48 |
| DE35 | FAIR | " | 23/10/43 | 17/11/45 | US Army, sold 1949 |
| DE36 | MANLOVE | " | 8/11/43 | 16/11/45 | Scrapped 3/48 |
| DE37 | GRIENER | PSNY | 18/ 8/43 | 19/11/45 | Scrapped 3/47 |
| DE38 | WYMAN | " | 1/ 9/43 | 21/12/45 | Scrapped 6/47 |

*This amidships close-up of the* ***USS EDWARD C. DALY DE17*** *taken on March 3, 1945 clearly shows the newly installed MK52 director and added loud-speaker to her mast. In two years, this ship along with many other EVARTS class ships will be scrapped.* 19N79886

*With overhaul completed the* ***USS CANFIELD DE262*** *is getting ready to get back into the war with newly added additions. The new items are circled in white. The* ***USS WESSON DE184*** *is in the background in this May 21, 1945 shot.* *19N84882*

*The aft section of the* ***USS CANFIELD DE262*** *shows the newly installed 40mm quad gun, which added a lot more fire power over the twin 40mm or 1.1"gun. Fitted with four 25-man balsa life rafts and floater nets, this was the extent of lifesaving equipment other than the 26' motor whale-boat and life jackets.* *19N84884*

| | | | | | |
|---|---|---|---|---|---|
| DE39 | LOVERING | " | 17/ 9/43 | 16/10/45 | Scrapped 1/47 |
| DE40 | SANDERS | " | 1/10/43 | 12/12/45 | Scrapped 6/47 |
| DE41 | BRACKETT | " | 18/10/43 | 23/11/45 | Scrapped 6/47 |
| DE42 | REYNOLDS | " | 1/11/43 | 5/12/45 | Scrapped 5/47 |
| DE43 | MITCHELL | " | 17/11/43 | 29/12/45 | Scrapped 1/47 |
| DE45 | ANDRES | PHNY | 15/ 3/43 | 18/10/45 | Scrapped 2/46 |
| DE47 | DECKER | " | 4/12/43 | 22/10/45 | China, lost 11/54 |
| DE48 | DOBLER | " | 17/ 5/43 | 2/10/45 | Scrapped 7/46 |
| DE49 | DONEFF | " | 10/ 6/43 | 2/12/45 | Scrapped 1/47 |
| DE50 | ENGSTROM | " | 21/ 6/43 | 19/12/45 | Scrapped 1/47 |
| DE256 | SEID | BosNY | 11/ 6/43 | 7/12/45 | Scrapped 2/47 |
| DE257 | SMARTT | " | 18/ 6/43 | 5/10/45 | Scrapped 8/46 |
| DE258 | W.S.BROWN | " | 25/ 6/43 | 4/10/45 | Scrapped 8/46 |
| DE259 | W.C.MILLER | " | 2/ 7/43 | 17/12/45 | Scrapped 5/47 |
| DE260 | CABANA | " | 9/ 7/43 | 9/ 1/46 | Scrapped 6/47 |
| DE261 | DIONNE | " | 16/ 7/43 | 18/ 1/46 | Scrapped 7/47 |
| DE262 | CANFIELD | " | 22/ 7/43 | 21/12/45 | Scrapped 7/47 |
| DE263 | DEEDE | " | 29/ 7/43 | 9/ 1/46 | Scrapped 7/47 |
| DE264 | ELDEN | " | 4/ 8/43 | 18/ 1/46 | Scrapped 7/47 |
| DE265 | CLOUES | " | 10/ 8/43 | 26/11/45 | Scrapped 6/47 |
| DE301 | LAKE | MINY | 5/ 2/44 | 3/12/46 | Scrapped 1/47 |
| DE302 | LYMAN | " | 19/ 2/44 | 5/12/46 | Scrapped 1/47 |
| DE303 | CROWLEY | " | 25/ 3/45 | 3/12/45 | Scrapped 1/47 |
| DE304 | RALL | " | 8/ 4/44 | 11/12/45 | Scrapped 4/47 |
| DE305 | HALLORAN | " | 27/ 5/44 | 2/11/45 | Scrapped 4/47 |
| DE306 | CONNOLLY | " | 8/ 7/44 | 22/11/45 | Scrapped 6/46 |
| DE307 | FINNEGAN | " | 19/ 8/44 | 27/11/45 | Scrapped 6/46 |
| DE527 | O'TOOLE | BosNY | 22/ 1/44 | 18/10/45 | Scrapped 3/46 |
| DE528 | J.J.POWERS | " | 29/ 2/44 | 16/10/45 | Scrapped 2/46 |
| DE529 | MASON | " | 20/ 3/44 | 12/10/45 | Scrapped 4/47 |
| DE530 | J.M.BERMINGHAM | " | 8/ 4/44 | 12/10/45 | Scrapped 3/46 |

*The USS **GILMORE DE18** is finished with her overhaul and is getting ready to join her sisters in the Pacific war. Newly added guns and directors will soon be aimed at the enemy. This photograph was taken at Mare Island on 3 March 1945.* 19N80083

*Taking on supplies at Mare Island in April, 1944, the **USS CROWLEY DE303** is shown here with the **USS SAN DIEGO CL(AA)53** in the background. Still carrying 1.1" guns which were replaced on most Destroyer Escorts as stock of the new 40mm guns became available.* 19N131503

# BUCKLEY CLASS

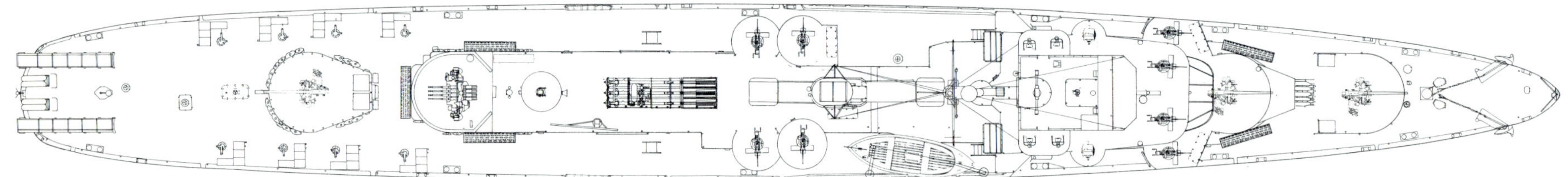

**USS ENGLAND DE635**
**February 1944**

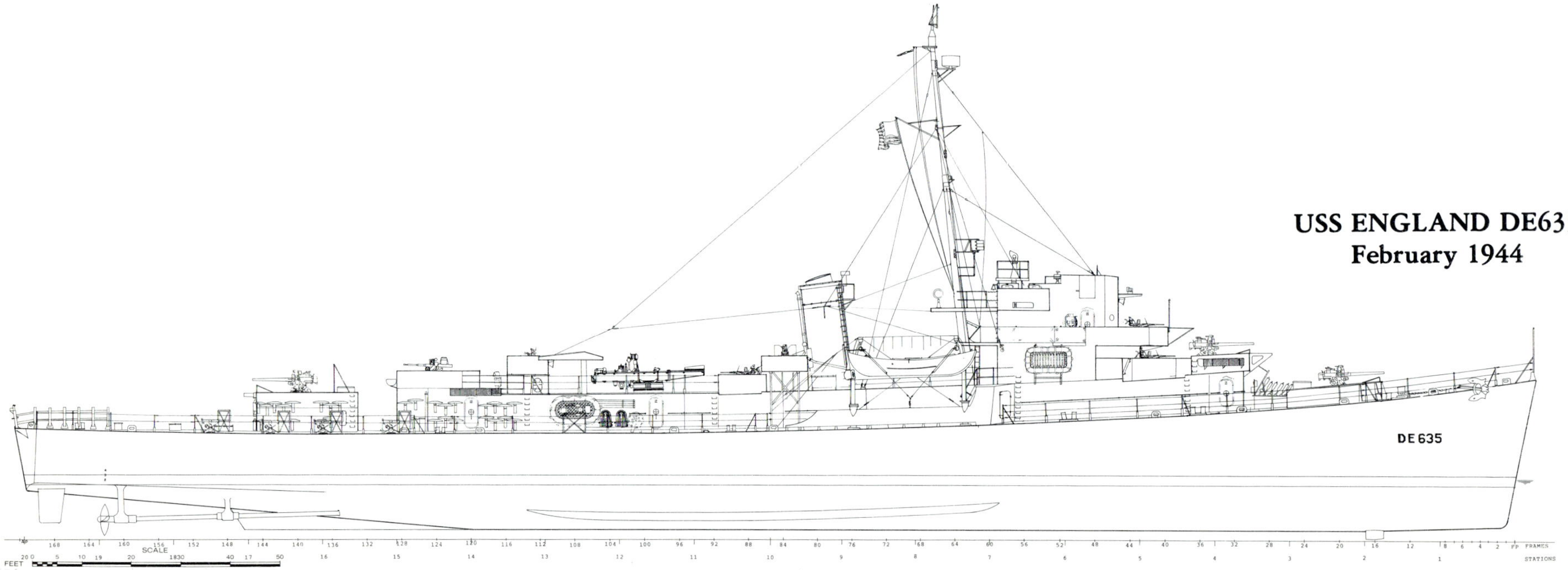

*In dazzle camouflage the **USS PAUL G. BAKER DE642** heads out to sea in this July 1944 photograph. This disruption type of camouflage was effective against submarines being able to get a good quick identification on its target.* USN

## BUCKLEY Class

**DE53-54, 56-57, 59,60, 62-63, 65-66, 68-70, 153-161, 198-223, 575-578, 633-644, 665-667, 675-683, 693-705, 789-800**

### GENERAL INFORMATION

| | |
|---|---|
| Length Overall | 306'-0" |
| Length at Waterline | 283'-6" |
| Beam | 36'-9" |
| Shaft Horsepower | 12,000 |
| Trail Speed | 23,7 Knots |
| War Endurance | 4,940 Miles/12 Knots |
| Displacement | 1,673 Tons |
| Complement | 15 Officers 198 Men |
| Fuel Capacity | 350 Tons |

### ARMAMENT

3-3"/50 Cal guns-Main Battery
1-Twin 40mm gun or 1-1.1" gun
8-20mm guns
1-Triple Torpedo Tube
1-Hedgehog
2-Depth Charge Tracks
8-"K" gun projectors

A total of 148 ships of this class were built during the war. Forty six going to Lend-Lease before commissioning into the US Navy. Unlike the "EVARTS," these ships, like the remaining classes of Destroyer Escorts built were of the Long Hull design (306'). The extra length was due to the needed room for planned steam power plants which gave the class the designed 12,000 shaft horsepower. With a Turbine-Electric Drive, this class was known as the "TE" class.

The first unit to be completed for the US Navy was the USS REUBEN JAMES DE153. It was built by the Norfolk Navy Yard and commissioned on April 1, 1943 with LCDR F.D. Giambattista, commanding. Unlike the "EVARTS," these ships were designed with a triple set of torpedo tubes mounted on the first superstructure deck amidships. This class experienced a wide range of armament changes. In the Fall of 1944, it was decided to convert these to carry the 5" gun rather than the 3" which they already carried. However by November 1944, the number of ships to be converted was cut back and by mid 1945 only 40 ships were slated for conversion. But, in fact only 11 were converted by late 1945.

The secondary battery were changed during the war for the need of more effective anti-aircraft defense. Four "TE's" (DE575-578) were completed without the triple torpedo tubes and were fitted with 4 single Army 40mm guns. These guns were added to the amidships location of the torpedo tubes. Other ships had this change made during the war when the ships had overhaul periods. Also, 2 more 20mm guns were added to the stern in tubes, for a total of 10-20mm guns.

In May 1944, 50 "TE's" were approved for conversion to APD's (High Speed Transports). DE668-673, which were still under construction were included in this fifty. However, only 37 units were converted to APD's. The need for Radar Picket Ships saw 5 "TE's" being converted for this role. Also, 4 were converted to Floating Power-Plants, with large cable reels installed amidships. These ships were used to supply power to an amphibious landing area.

The **BUCKLEYS** were more successful than the **EVARTS.** These ships were saved for use in the post war navy, both active and reserve. By 1960 only 1 ship served with Fleet units on active status. Ten were given to Foreign navies during the 1960's and some were still in-service as of 1986.

## BUCKLEY (TE) CLASS

| | | | | | |
|---|---|---|---|---|---|
| DE51 | BUCKLEY | BethHI | 30/ 4/43 | 3/ 7/46 | DER, sold 1969 |
| DE53 | C.LAWRENCE | " | 31/ 5/43 | | APD37(10/44) Scrapped 9/64 |
| DE54 | D.T.GRIFFIN | " | 9/ 6/43 | 30/ 5/46 | Scrapped APD38(10/44) |
| DE56 | DONNELL | " | 26/ 6/43 | 23/10/45 | IX182(7/44) sold 4/46 |
| DE57 | FOGG | " | 7/ 7/43 | 27/10/47 | DER, sold 1/66 |
| DE59 | FOSS | " | 23/ 7/43 | 30/10/57 | Target 11/65 |
| DE60 | GANTNER | " | 23/ 7/43 | 2/ 8/49 | APD42(2/45) China 2/66 |
| DE62 | G.W.INGRAM | " | 11/ 8/43 | 15/ 1/47 | APD43(2/45) Sold 1/67 |
| DE63 | IRA JEFFERY | " | 15/ 8/43 | 18/ 6/46 | APD44(2/45) Sunk test 7/62 |
| DE65 | LEE FOX | " | 30/ 8/43 | 13/ 5/46 | APD45(2/45) Scrapped 1/66 |
| DE66 | AMESBURY | " | 31/ 8/43 | 3/ 7/46 | APD46(2/45) Discarded 1960 |
| DE68 | BATES | " | 12/ 9/43 | | APD47(7/44) Sunk 25/5/45 |
| DE69 | BLESSMAN | " | 19/ 9/43 | 15/ 1/47 | APD48(7/44) |
| DE70 | J.E.CAMPBELL | " | 23/ 9/43 | 15/11/46 | APD49(7/44) Chile 11/66 |
| DE153 | REUBEN JAMES | NorNY | 1/ 4/43 | 11/10/47 | DER(45) target 68-71 |
| DE154 | SIMS | " | 24/ 4/43 | 24/ 4/46 | APD50(9/44) Scrapped 4/61 |
| DE155 | HOPPING | " | 21/ 5/43 | 5/ 5/47 | APD51(9/44) Scrapped 8/66 |
| DE156 | REEVES | " | 9/ 6/43 | 30/ 7/46 | APD52(9/44) Ecuador 6/60 |

| | | | | | |
|---|---|---|---|---|---|
| DE157 | FECHTELER | ” | 1/ 7/43 | | Lost 4/5/44 |
| DE158 | CHASE | ” | 18/ 7/43 | 15/ 1/46 | APD54(11/44) Scrapped 11/46 |
| DE159 | LANING | ” | 1/ 8/43 | 13/ 9/57 | APD55(11/44) LPR55 (1/69) |
| DE160 | LOY | ” | 12/ 9/43 | 21/ 2/47 | APD56(11/44) Scrapped 8/66 |
| DE161 | BARBER | ” | 10/10/43 | 22/ 5/46 | APD57(11/44) |
| DE198 | LOVELACE | ” | 7/11/43 | 22/ 5/46 | Target 4/68 |
| DE199 | MANNING | ChrNY | 1/10/43 | 15/ 1/47 | Scrapped 8/68 |
| DE200 | NEUENDORF | ” | 18/10/43 | 14/ 5/46 | Scrapped 11/67 |
| DE201 | J.E.CRAIG | ” | 1/11/43 | 2/ 7/46 | Target 2/69 |
| DE202 | EICHENBERGER | ” | 19/11/43 | 14/ 5/46 | Scrapped 1972 |
| DE203 | THOMASON | ” | 10/12/43 | 22/ 5/46 | Scrapped 1968 |
| DE204 | JORDAN | ” | 17/12/43 | 19/12/45 | Collision(7/45) Scrapped 1947 |
| DE205 | NEWMAN | ” | 26/11/43 | 18/ 2/46 | Scrapped 8/66 |
| DE206 | LIDDLE | ” | 6/12/43 | 18/ 3/67 | APD60(7/44) Scrapped 6/67 |
| DE207 | KEPHART | ” | 7/ 1/44 | 21/ 6/46 | Korea 5/67 |
| DE208 | COFER | ” | 19/ 1/44 | 28/ 6/46 | APD62(7/44) |
| DE209 | LLOYD | ” | 11/ 2/44 | 18/ 2/58 | APD63(7/44) Scrapped 6/66 |
| DE210 | OTTER | ” | 21/ 2/44 | 1/ /47 | Target 7/70 |

| | | | | | |
|---|---|---|---|---|---|
| DE211 | J.C.HUBBARD | ” | 6/ 3/44 | 15/ 3/46 | APD53(6/45) Scrapped 5/66 |
| DE212 | HAYTER | ” | 16/ 3/44 | 19/ 3/46 | APD80(6/45) Scrapped 1/67 |
| DE213 | W.T.POWELL | ” | 28/ 3/44 | 17/ 1/58 | DER(45) Scrapped 10/66 |
| DE214 | SCOTT | PHNY | 20/ 7/43 | 3/ 3/47 | Scrapped 1/67 |
| DE215 | BURKE | ” | 20/ 8/43 | 22/ 6/49 | APD65(1/45) |
| DE216 | ENRIGHT | ” | 21/ 9/43 | 21/ 6/46 | APD66(1/45) |
| DE217 | COOLBAUGH | ” | 15/10/43 | 21/ 2/59 | Scrapped 73 |
| DE218 | DARBY | ” | 15/11/43 | / /58 | NRF59-62 Target 5/70 |
| DE219 | J.D.BLACKWOOD | ” | 15/12/43 | 1/ 8/58 | NRF58-70 Target 7/70 |
| DE220 | F.M.ROBINSON | ” | 15/ 1/44 | 20/ 6/60 | Scrapped 8/72 |
| DE221 | SOLAR | ” | 15/ 2/44 | | Scuttled 6/46 |
| DE222 | FOWLER | ” | 15/ 3/44 | 28/ 6/46 | Scrapped 67 |
| DE223 | SPANGENBERG | ” | 15/ 4/44 | 18/10/47 | DER(45) Scrapped 10/66 |
| DE575 | AHRENS | BethHI | 12/ 2/44 | 24/ 6/46 | Scrapped 6/67 |
| DE576 | BARR | ” | 15/ 2/44 | 12/ 7/46 | APD39(7/44) Scrapped 60 |
| DE577 | A.J.LUKE | ” | 19/ 2/44 | 18/10/47 | DER(45) Target 10/70 |
| DE578 | R.I.PAINE | ” | 26/ 2/44 | 21/11/47 | DER(45) Sold 68 |
| DE633 | FOREMAN | BethSF | 22/10/43 | 28/ 6/46 | Scrapped 6/65 |
| DE634 | WHITEHURST | ” | 19/11/43 | 25/ 7/65 | NRF Target 7/69 |
| DE635 | ENGLAND | ” | 10/12/43 | 15/10/45 | Scrapped 1945 |

*A good overhead view of the* ***USS COFFER DE208*** *taken from 300' shows her gun arrangement and depth charge layout. Equipped with a HF-DF antenna on her stub mast while she carries a "SA" radar antenna on her foremast. This view was taken in May 1944 off New York.* *19N64222*

*This Atlantic fleet ship, the* ***USS OTTER DE210*** *shows her HF-DF direction gear mounted atop her aft mast. Very effective against submarines during the Atlantic campaign. Also, she is carrying a "SA" radar atop her main mast in this 1944 photograph.* *19N69445*

| DE636 | WITTER | ” | 29/12/43 | 29/10/45 | Scrapped 12/46 |
|---|---|---|---|---|---|
| DE637 | BOWERS | ” | 27/ 1/44 | 18/12/58 | APD40(6/45) Philippine 4/61 |
| DE638 | WILLMARTH | ” | 13/ 3/44 | 26/ 4/46 | Scrapped 7/68 |
| DE639 | GENDREAU | ” | 17/ 3/44 | 13/ 3/48 | Scrapped 73 |
| DE640 | FIEBERLING | ” | 11/ 4/44 | 13/ 3/48 | Scrapped 72 |
| DE641 | W.C.COLE | ” | 12/ 5/44 | 3/ 2/47 | Scrapped 69 |
| DE642 | P.G.BAKER | ” | 25/ 5/44 | 3/ 2/47 | Scrapped 69 |

*Wearing measure 32 dazzle camouflage pattern the* ***USS WILLIAM C. COLE DE641*** *leaves the Bethlehem Steel Plant in San Francisco, after being built. This May 1944 photograph shows the beautiful lines of these vessels.*
*USN*

*Steaming out of Norfolk, the* ***USS HOPPING DE155*** *is heading for her first duty assignment. She is painted in a false waterline type of camouflage when this photograph was taken in July 1943. Note the small oval life raft mounted on the gun shield.*
*USN*

*This aerial view of the* **USS BURKE DE215** *loading supplies in June 1944 shows the arrangement of the 4 single 40mm guns mounted amidships. These guns replaced the triple torpedo tubes in favor of more anti-aircraft protection.* 19N66900

*Converted to an electric supply ship, the* **USS WISEMAN DE667** *shows the large cable reels added to her superstructure deck amidships.* 19N76912

| | | | | | |
|---|---|---|---|---|---|
| DE643 | D.M.CUMMINGS | " | 29/ 6/44 | 3/ 2/47 | Target 69 |
| DE644 | VAMMEN | " | 27/ 7/44 | 1/ 8/62 | NRF60-69 Target 7/69 |
| DE665 | JENKS | Dravo | 19/ 1/44 | 26/ 6/46 | Scrapped 9/68 |
| DE666 | DURIK | " | 24/ 3/44 | 15/ 6/46 | Scrapped 1/67 |
| DE667 | WISEMAN | " | 4/ 4/44 | 16/ 5/59 | NRF59-68 Scrapped 73 |
| DE675 | WEBER | BethQ | 30/ 6/43 | 15/ 1/47 | APD75(1/45) Target 7/62 |
| DE676 | SCHMITT | " | 24/ 7/43 | 28/ 6/49 | APD76(1/45) Taiwan 2/67 |
| DE677 | FRAMENT | " | 15/ 8/43 | 30/ 5/46 | APD77(1/45) |
| DE678 | HARMON | " | 31/ 8/43 | 25/ 3/47 | Scrapped 1/67 |
| DE679 | GREENWOOD | " | 25/ 9/43 | 1/ 8/62 | NRF62-67 Scrapped 2/67 |
| DE680 | LOESER | " | 10/10/43 | 22/ 9/68 | NRF Scrapped 9/68 |
| DE681 | GILLETTE | " | 27/10/43 | 12/46 | Scrapped 1/73 |
| DE682 | UNDERHILL | " | 15/11/43 | | Lost 24/7/45 |
| DE683 | H.R.KENYON | " | 30/11/43 | 3/ 2/47 | Scrapped 12/69 |
| DE693 | BULL | Defoe | 12/ 8/43 | 5/ 6/47 | APD78(7/44) |
| DE694 | BUNCH | " | 21/ 8/43 | 31/ 5/46 | APD79(7/44) |
| DE695 | RICH | " | 1/10/43 | | Lost mine 8/6/44 |
| DE696 | SPANGLER | " | 31/10/43 | 8/10/58 | NRF Scrapped 11/69 |
| DE697 | GEORGE | " | 20/11/43 | 8/10/58 | NRF Scrapped 6/69 |
| DE698 | RABY | " | 7/12/43 | 22/12/53 | NRF Scrapped 6/68 |
| DE699 | MARSH | " | 12/ 1/44 | 16/ 8/58 | NRF58-69 |
| DE700 | CURRIER | " | 1/ 2/44 | 4/ 4/60 | Target 7/67 |
| DE701 | OSMUS | " | 17/ 8/43 | 15/ 3/47 | Scrapped 12/72 |
| DE702 | E.V.JOHNSON | " | 18/ 3/44 | 18/ 6/46 | Sold 9/68 |
| DE703 | HOLTON | " | 1/ 5/44 | 31/ 5/46 | Scrapped 11/71 |
| DE704 | CRONIN | " | 5/ 5/44 | 31/ 5/46 | Scrapped 70 |
| DE705 | FRYBARGER | " | 18/ 5/44 | 9/12/54 | Scrapped 12/72 |
| DE789 | TATUM | Cons | 22/11/43 | 15/11/46 | APD81(12/44) Scrapped 5/61 |
| DE790 | BORUM | " | 30/11/43 | 15/ 6/46 | Scrapped 4/67 |
| DE791 | MALOY | " | 13/12/43 | 28/ 5/65 | Sold 3/66 |
| DE792 | HAINES | " | 27/12/43 | 29/ 4/46 | APD84(12/44) Scrapped 5/61 |
| DE793 | RUNELS | " | 3/ 1/44 | 10/ 2/47 | APD85(12/45) Scrapped 62 |
| DE794 | HOLLIS | " | 24/ 1/44 | 16/10/56 | APD86(12/44) |
| DE795 | GUNASON | " | 1/ 2/44 | 13/ 3/48 | Target 7/74 |
| DE796 | MAJOR | " | 12/ 2/44 | 13/ 3/48 | Sold 11/73 |
| DE797 | WEEDEN | " | 19/ 2/44 | 26/ 2/58 | NRF56-50 Sold 10/69 |
| DE798 | VARIAN | " | 29/ 2/44 | 15/ 3/46 | Sold 1/74 |
| DE799 | SCROGGINS | " | 30/ 3/44 | 28/ 2/47 | Sold 4/67 |
| DE800 | J.W.WILKE | " | 7/ 3/44 | 24/ 5/60 | Sold 2/74 |

*Wearing three colors of paint the* **USS DAMON M. CUMMINGS DE643** *shows the effect of this type of camouflage. Newly completed she is shown here in July 1944 leaving the building yards at San Francisco.*
*19N68094*

This stern aerial view of the **USS ROBERT I. PAINE DE578** was taken in July 1944. Equipped with army 40mm gun for added defense against aircraft. She still carries the 1.1" gun aft.
80G237138

*Heading down the Delaware River after leaving Philadelphia Navy Yard, in the summer of 1943, the* **USS BURKE DE215** *is a typical Buckley class Destroyer Escort. The* **BURKE** *was converted to an APD in January 1945.*
*USN*

*Another Philadelphia-built Escort is the* **USS J. DOUGLAS BLACKWOOD DE219**, *shown here in January 1946, leaving Mare Island with newly added 5" guns. These 5" guns added a bigger punch to the fire power of these ships. Also, note the extension of her forward part of the bridge.*

*An early postwar shot of the* **USS DARBY DE218.** *Addition of the 5" gun moved the hedgehog launcher to the 01 level. Also, additional 40mm guns were added and the torpedo tubes were removed.*
*19N91293*

# RUDDEROW CLASS

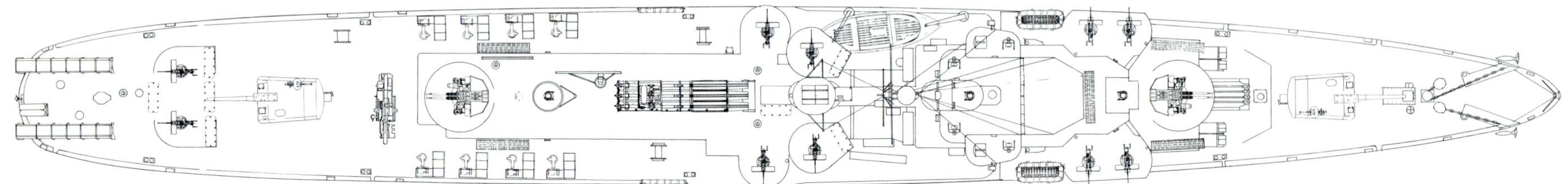

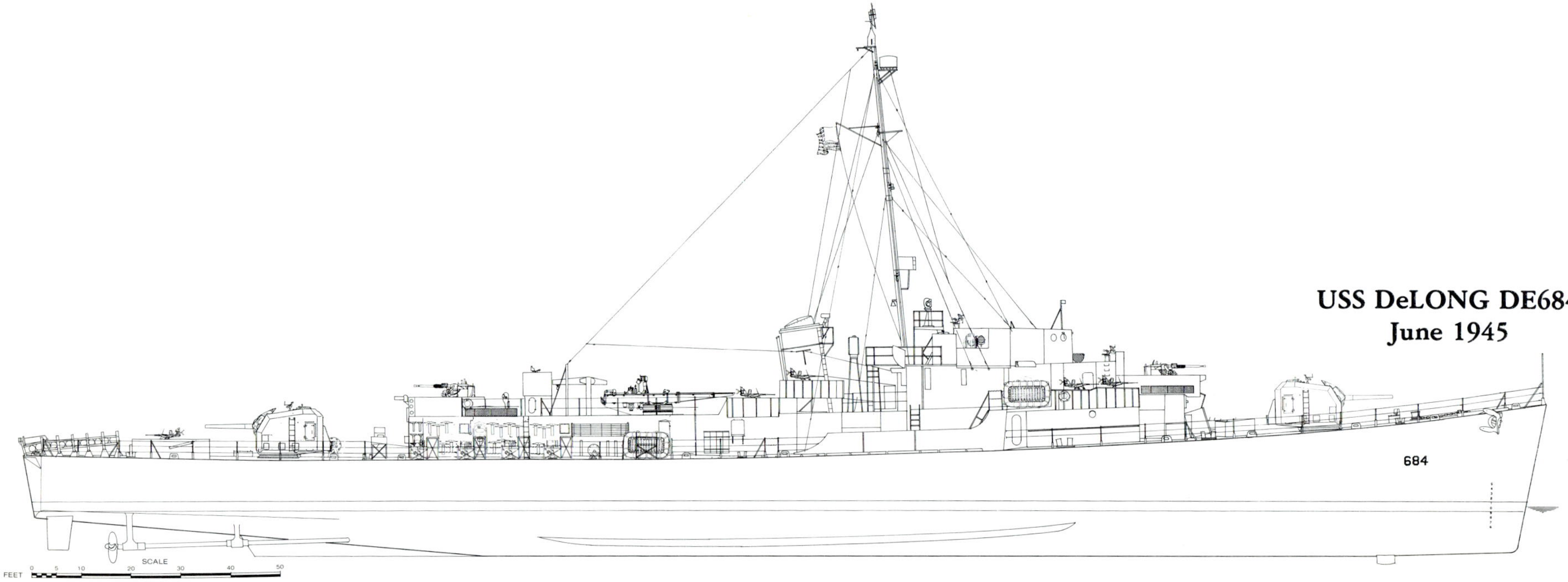

**USS DeLONG DE684**
**June 1945**

*Sailing down the calm Delaware River in May 1944. The* ***USS RUDDEROW DE224,*** *namesake of the class, leaves the Philadelphia Navy Yard. Fitted with a cut-down bridge and 5" guns this class saw only 22 units built as Destroyer Escorts. Another 50 were built as APD's.* USN

## RUDDEROW Class

**DE224-225, 230-231, 579-589, 706-709**

### GENERAL INFORMATION

| | |
|---|---|
| Length Overall | 306'-0" |
| Length at Waterline | 300'-0" |
| Beam | 36'-11" |
| Shaft Horsepower | 12,000 |
| Trail Speed | 24 Knots |
| War Endurance | 5,050 Miles/12 Knots |
| Displacement | 1,450 Tons |
| Complement | 12 Officers 192 Men |
| Fuel Capacity | 354.5 Tons |

### ARMAMENT

2-5"/38 cal guns-Main Battery
2-Twin 40mm gun
1-Triple Torpedo Tube
10-20mm guns
1-Hedgehog
2-Depth Charge Tracks
8-"K" gun projectors

A total of 72 ships of this class were built. However, only 22 ships were commissioned as Destroyer Escorts. The rest were completed as APD's. An additional 83 ships were cancelled from the building program in 1943 and 1944.

This class was also known as the "TEV" due to having Turbine-Electric-Drive like the **BUCKLEYS.** This **LONG HULL** mounted the 5"/38 cal gun to an enclosed single mount and a new lower bridge superstructure. The first ship of this class to be built was the **USS DeLONG DE684.** It was built at Bethlehem Steel Yard in Quincy and commissioned on December 31, 1943, with LCDR R.C. Houston commanding. These ships served in the US Navy reserve fleet after the war and two were transferred to foreign navies in the 1960's.

RUDDEROW (TEV) CLASS

| | | | | | |
|---|---|---|---|---|---|
| DE224 | RUDDEROW | PHNY | 15/ 5/44 | 15/ 1/46 | Sold 6/68 |
| DE225 | DAY | " | 10/ 1/44 | 15/ 5/46 | Target 3/69 |
| DE230 | CHAFFEE | CharNY | 9/ 5/44 | 15/ 4/46 | Sold 6/48 |
| DE231 | HODGES | " | 27/ 5/44 | 22/ 6/46 | Sold 73 |
| DE579 | RILEY | BethHI | 13/ 3/44 | 15/ 1/47 | Taiwan 7/68 |
| DE580 | L.B.KNOX | " | 22/ 3/44 | 15/ 6/46 | Sold 1/72 |
| DE581 | McNULTY | " | 31/ 3/44 | 2/ 6/46 | Sold 1/72 |
| DE582 | METIVIER | " | 7/ 4/44 | 1/ 6/46 | Sold 5/69 |
| DE583 | G.A.JOHNSON | " | 15/ 4/44 | 31/ 5/46 | Sold 9/66 |
| DE584 | C.J.KIMMEL | " | 20/ 4/44 | 15/ 1/47 | Target 11/69 |
| DE585 | D.A.JOY | " | 28/ 4/44 | 65 | NRF Sold 3/66 |
| DE586 | LOUGH | " | 2/ 5/44 | 24/ 6/46 | Sold 69 |
| DE587 | T.F.NICKEL | " | 9/ 6/44 | 22/ 2/58 | NRF Sold 12/72 |
| DE588 | PEIFFER | " | 15/ 6/44 | 1/ 6/46 | Target 5/67 |
| DE589 | TINSMAN | " | 26/ 6/44 | 11/ 5/46 | Sold 5/72 |
| DE684 | DE LONG | BethQ | 31/12/43 | 8/ 8/69 | NRF Target 2/70 |
| DE685 | COATES | " | 24/ 1/44 | 30/ 1/70 | NRF Target 9/71 |
| DE686 | E.E.ELMORE | " | 4/ 2/44 | 31/ 5/46 | Sold 5/69 |
| DE706 | HOLT | Defoe | 9/ 6/44 | 2/ 7/46 | Korea 6/63 |
| DE707 | JOBB | " | 4/ 7/44 | 13/ 5/46 | Sold 11/69 |
| DE708 | PARLE | " | 29/ 7/44 | 7/62 | NRF Target 10/70 |
| DE709 | BRAY | " | 4/ 9/44 | 10/ 5/46 | APD139(7/45) Target 3/63 |

*Wearing camouflage measure 32 design 3D the **USS TINSMAN DE589** is leaving Boston Navy Yard in September 1944. She is fitted with an HF-DF antenna aft.* *USN*

*Lacking her "SA" radar or HF-DF antenna the **USS McNULTY DE581** is photographed in Boston Harbor in April 1944. This class had Turbo-electric drive and could do 24 knots.* *19N68391*

*Given to Taiwan in 1969 the **USS RILEY DE579** is shown here in March 1944 leaving Boston. She is wearing measure 22 camouflage.* *19N68395*

# Typical BUCKLEY Class

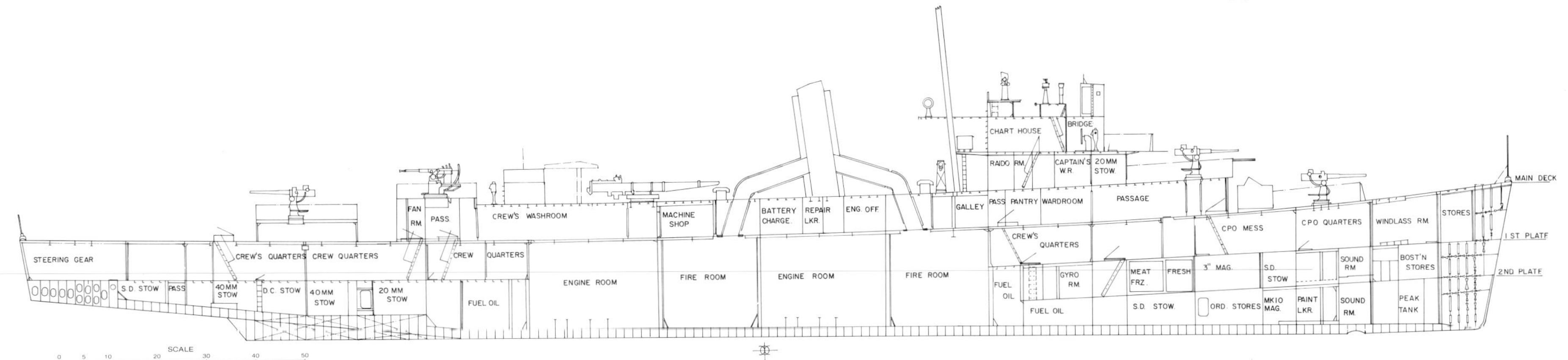


INBOARD PROFILE

TYPICAL DESTROYER ESCORT

*SAMUEL B. ROBERTS DE413, 1944, measure 32 design 22D*

*BAKER DE642 in 1944 in measure 32 design 22D camouflage.*

*DeLONG DE684 in 1945 in measure 21 camouflage overall Navy Blue.*

*USS BUCKLEY DE51, 1943, measure 22 camouflage.*

*USS*

*USS HARDY DE20, 1943 in measure 14 camouflage overall Ocean Gray.*

*USS*

*USS LEVY DE162, June 1943 in measure 22 camouflage.*

*USS*

*Close-up of an unknown Destroyer Escort at Mare Island in April 1945. These two views show the little-seen bridge details. A MK52 director is installed forward of the mast and lookout chairs abreast the bridge. The captain's chair can be seen on the starboard side.* USN

*USS PETTIT DE253, May 1944 in measure 22 camouflage.*

*USS GANTNER APD42 in the big pattern jungle camouflage.*

*USS CROSLEY APD 87 in October 1944 in small pattern jungle camouflage.*

# CANNON CLASS

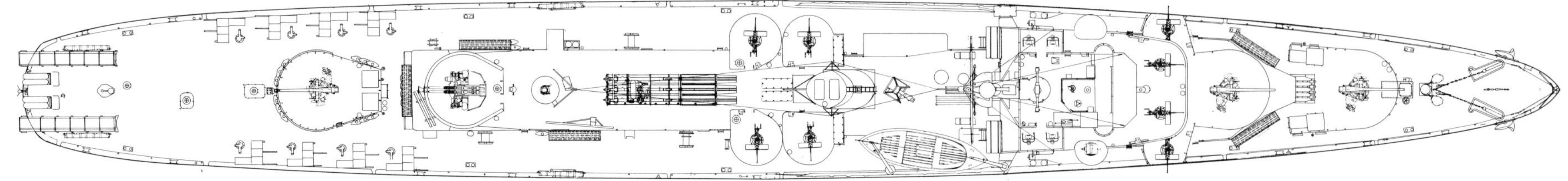

**USS SWEARER DE186**
**February 1944**

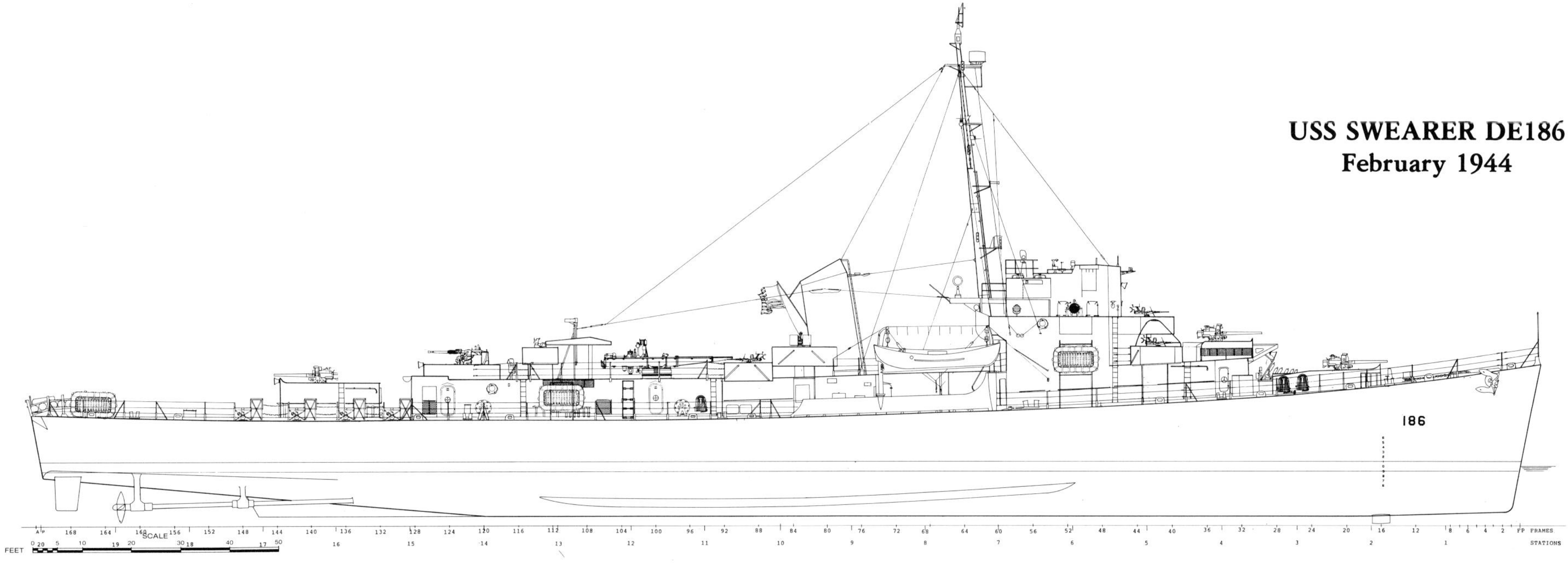

# Where the DE's Are

Most of the 565 destroyer escorts that were constructed between 1943 and 1945 have been scrapped or sunk as practice targets. However, four decades later, a number of them remain in active servie in foreign navies.

Interest in the surviving ships reached a peak as a result of the visit of the HURST DE-250 (Mexico's COMODORO MANUEL AZUETA) to the Port of Philadelphia during our recent convention. Many of our members wanted to know which ships still existed and where they were.

In response, the accompanying chart was developed. Information was obtained from several readers and a variety of printed sources such as annual issues of *Janes Fighting Ships* through 1986-87, *Escort Ships of the World* by B. Ireland (1979) and *American Fleet and Escort Destroyers* by H.T. Lenton (1973).

Through use of several sources of different time periods, we were able to trace the ships to their present destinations and to learn of the deletion other ships that ended up in foreign countries. In addition, we came across items of interest such as the ENRIGHT (DE-216) (Ecuador) being modified to carry a helicopter, the WATERMAN (DE-740) and WEAVER (DE-741) (both in Peru) being respectively used as a floating power station and submarine accommodation ship. Another intriguing item: the RUCHAMKIN (DE-228/APD-66) (Colombia) was reported in 1980 to be on exhibit in Bogota; it may be in existence in a museum capacity this day. Also, the FORSTER (DE-334) was captured as South Vietnam fell and is now operating in Vietnam as Trans Khan Du.

| Ship | DE No. | APD No. | Year Transferred | Name | Number | | Remarks |
|---|---|---|---|---|---|---|---|
| **CHILE** | | | | | | | |
| Daniel T. Griffin | 54 | 38 | 1967 | Virgilio Uribe | PF-29 | A | |
| Joseph E. Campbell | 70 | 49 | 1966 | Riquelme | | A | Used for parts |
| Odum | 670 | 71 | 1966 | Serrano | PF-26 | A | |
| Jack E. Robinson | 671 | 72 | 1966 | Orelia | PF-27 | A | |
| **COLOMBIA** | | | | | | | |
| Bassett | 672 | 73 | 1967 | Almirante Tono | DT-04 | A | |
| Ruchamkin | 228 | 89 | 1967 | Cordoba | DT-15 | A | |
| **ECUADOR** | | | | | | | |
| Enright | 216 | 66 | 1967 | Moran Valerde | | A-B | |
| **GREECE** | | | | | | | |
| Eldridge | 173 | — | 1951 | Leon | D-54 | A-B | |
| Elbert | 768 | — | 1951 | Ierax | D-31 | A-B | |
| Garfield Thomas | 193 | — | 1951 | Panthis | D-67 | A-B | |
| Slatter | 766 | — | 1951 | Aetos | D-01 | A-B | |
| **INONESIA** | | | | | | | |
| Begor | 711 | 127 | 1976 | Unnamed | | A | |
| Balduck | 716 | 132 | 1976 | Unnamed | | A | |
| **MEXICO** | | | | | | | |
| Hurst | 250 | — | 1973 | Comodoro Manuel Azueta | A-06 | A-B | |
| Joseph M. Auman | 674 | 117 | 1964 | Tehuantepec | B-05 | A-B | |
| Don O. Woods | 721 | 118 | 1964 | Usumacinta | B-06 | A-B | |
| Rednour | 592 | 102 | 1966 | Coahuila | B-07 | A-B | |
| Barber | 161 | 57 | | Chihuahua | B-08 | A-B | |
| **PERU** | | | | | | | |
| Weaver | 741 | — | 1951 | Rodriguez | DE-163 | A-B | |
| Bangust | 739 | — | 1952 | Castilla | DE-161 | A | Training ship Deleted 1980 |
| Waterman | 740 | — | 1952 | Aguirre | DE-162 | A-B | |
| **PHILIPPINES** | | | | | | | |
| Camp | 251 | — | 1976 | Rajah Lakandula | | A-B | From So. Vietnam |
| Amick | 168 | — | 1976 | Sikatuna | PF-5 | A-B | From Japan |
| Atherton | 169 | — | 1976 | Rajah Humabon | PF-6 | A-B | From Japan |
| Booth | 170 | — | 1968 | Datu Halantaw | PS-76 | A | Sunk 1981 |
| **SOUTH KOREA** | | | | | | | |
| Kephart | 207 | 61 | 1967 | Kyong Puk | 85 | A-B | |
| Cavallaro | 712 | 128 | 1959 | Kyong Nam | 81 | A-B | |
| Hayter | 212 | 80 | 1968 | Jon Nam | 86 | A-B | |
| Holt | 706 | — | 1963 | Chung Nam | | A | Deleted 1984 |
| Muir | 770 | — | 1956 | Kang Won | 72 | A | |
| Sutton | 771 | — | 1956 | Kyong Ki | 71 | A | |
| William M. Hobby | 236 | 95 | 1967 | Cheju | 87 | A-B | |
| Harry L. Corl | 598 | 108 | 1966 | Ah San | 82 | A | Deleted 1984 |
| Julius A. Raven | 600 | 110 | 1966 | Ung Po | 83 | A | Deleted 1984 |
| **TAIWAN** | | | | | | | |
| Riley | 579 | — | 1969 | Tai Yuan | 959 | A-B | |
| Kleinsmith | 718 | 134 | 1960 | Tien Shan | 615 | A-B | |
| Kinzer | 232 | 921 | 1966 | Yu Shan | 826 | A-B | |
| Bull | 693 | 78 | 1966 | Lu Shan | 821 | A-B | |
| Gantner | 60 | 42 | 1966 | Wen Shan | 834 | A-B | |
| Truxton | 282 | 98 | 1966 | Fu Shan | 838 | A-B | |
| Blessman | 69 | 48 | 1967 | Chung Shan | 845 | A-B | |
| Donald W. Wolf | 713 | 129 | 1968 | Hua Shan | 854 | A-B | |
| Register | 233 | 92 | 1966 | Tai Shan | 878 | A-B | |
| Kline | 687 | 120 | 1966 | Shou Shan | 893 | A-B | |
| Raymond W. Herndon | 688 | 121 | 1967 | Chung Nam | | A | |
| George W. Ingram | 62 | 43 | | Kang Shan | | A | |
| **THAILAND** | | | | | | | |
| Hemminger | 746 | | 1959 | Pin Klao | | A-B | |
| **TUNISIA** | | | | | | | |
| Thomas J. Gary | 326 | | 1973 | President Bourguiba | | A-B | |
| **URUGUAY** | | | | | | | |
| Baron | 166 | | 1952 | Uruguay | 1 | A-B | |
| Bronstein | 189 | | 1952 | Artigas | 2 | A-B | |
| **VIET NAM** | | | | | | | |
| Forster | 334 | | 1975 | Trans Khan Du | | A-B | |
| **BRAZIL** | | | | | | | |
| McAnn | 179 | — | 1944 | Bracui | | | Museum Ship Rio de Janiero |
| **UNITED STATES** | | | | | | | |
| Stewart | 238 | | | Stewart | 238 | | Museum Ship Galveston, Texas |

**Explanation:**
A — Active 1979
B — Active 1986

It is the Rising Sun on the *Hatsuhi*, formerly the ATHERTON (DE-169). It was transferred to the Philippines and is now the *Rajah Humabon*.

# Where the DE's Are

Most of the 565 destroyer escorts that were constructed between 1943 and 1945 have been scrapped or sunk as practice targets. However, four decades later, a number of them remain in active servie in foreign navies.

Interest in the surviving ships reached a peak as a result of the visit of the HURST DE-250 (Mexico's COMODORO MANUEL AZUETA) to the Port of Philadelphia during our recent convention. Many of our members wanted to know which ships still existed and where they were.

In response, the accompanying chart was developed. Information was obtained from several readers and a variety of printed sources such as annual issues of *Janes Fighting Ships* through 1986-87, *Escort Ships of the World* by B. Ireland (1979) and *American Fleet and Escort Destroyers* by H.T. Lenton (1973).

Through use of several sources of different time periods, we were able to trace the ships to their present destinations and to learn of the deletion other ships that ended up in foreign countries. In addition, we came across items of interest such as the ENRIGHT (DE-216) (Ecuador) being modified to carry a helicopter, the WATERMAN (DE-740) and WEAVER (DE-741) (both in Peru) being respectively used as a floating power station and submarine accommodation ship. Another intriguing item: the RUCHAMKIN (DE-228/APD-66) (Colombia) was reported in 1980 to be on exhibit in Bogota; it may be in existence in a museum capacity this day. Also, the FORSTER (DE-334) was captured as South Vietnam fell and is now operating in Vietnam as Trans Khan Du.

| Ship | DE No. | APD No. | Year Transferred | Name | Number | | Remarks |
|---|---|---|---|---|---|---|---|
| **CHILE** | | | | | | | |
| Daniel T. Griffin | 54 | 38 | 1967 | Virgilio Uribe | PF-29 | A | |
| Jospeh E. Campbell | 70 | 49 | 1966 | Riquelme | | A | Used for parts |
| Odum | 670 | 71 | 1966 | Serrano | PF-26 | A | |
| Jack E. Robinson | 671 | 72 | 1966 | Orelia | PF-27 | A | |
| **COLOMBIA** | | | | | | | |
| Bassett | 672 | 73 | 1967 | Almirante Tono | DT-04 | A | |
| Ruchamkin | 228 | 89 | 1967 | Cordoba | DT-15 | A | |
| **ECUADOR** | | | | | | | |
| Enright | 216 | 66 | 1967 | Moran Valerde | | A-B | |
| **GREECE** | | | | | | | |
| Eldridge | 173 | — | 1951 | Leon | D-54 | A-B | |
| Elbert | 768 | — | 1951 | Ierax | D-31 | A-B | |
| Garfield Thomas | 193 | — | 1951 | Panthis | D-67 | A-B | |
| Slatter | 766 | — | 1951 | Aetos | D-01 | A-B | |
| **INONESIA** | | | | | | | |
| Begor | 711 | 127 | 1976 | Unnamed | | A | |
| Balduck | 716 | 132 | 1976 | Unnamed | | A | |
| **MEXICO** | | | | | | | |
| Hurst | 250 | — | 1973 | Comodoro Manuel Azueta | A-06 | A-B | |
| Joseph M. Auman | 674 | 117 | 1964 | Tehuantepec | B-05 | A-B | |
| Don O. Woods | 721 | 118 | 1964 | Usumacinta | B-06 | A-B | |
| Rednour | 592 | 102 | 1966 | Coahuila | B-07 | A-B | |
| Barber | 161 | 57 | | Chihuahua | B-08 | A-B | |
| **PERU** | | | | | | | |
| Weaver | 741 | — | 1951 | Rodriguez | DE-163 | A-B | |
| Bangust | 739 | — | 1952 | Castilla | DE-161 | A | Training ship Deleted 1980 |
| Waterman | 740 | — | 1952 | Aguirre | DE-162 | A-B | |
| **PHILIPPINES** | | | | | | | |
| Camp | 251 | — | 1976 | Rajah Lakandula | | A-B | From So. Vietnam |
| Amick | 168 | — | 1976 | Sikatuna | PF-5 | A-B | From Japan |
| Atherton | 169 | — | 1976 | Rajah Humabon | PF-6 | A-B | From Japan |
| Booth | 170 | — | 1968 | Datu Halanuaw | PS-76 | A | Sunk 1981 |
| **SOUTH KOREA** | | | | | | | |
| Kephart | 207 | 61 | 1967 | Kyong Puk | 85 | A-B | |
| Cavallaro | 712 | 128 | 1959 | Kyong Nam | 81 | A-B | |
| Hayter | 212 | 80 | 1968 | Jon Nam | 86 | A-B | |
| Holt | 706 | — | 1963 | Chung Nam | | A | Deleted 1984 |
| Muir | 770 | — | 1956 | Kang Won | 72 | A | |
| Sutton | 771 | — | 1956 | Kyong Ki | 71 | A | |
| William M. Hobby | 236 | 95 | 1967 | Cheju | 87 | A-B | |
| Harry L. Corl | 598 | 108 | 1966 | Ah San | 82 | A | Deleted 1984 |
| Julius A. Raven | 600 | 110 | 1966 | Ung Po | 83 | A | Deleted 1984 |

| Ship | DE No. | APD No. | Year Transferred | Name | Number | | Remarks |
|---|---|---|---|---|---|---|---|
| **TAIWAN** | | | | | | | |
| Riley | 579 | — | 1969 | Tai Yuan | 959 | A-B | |
| Kleinsmith | 718 | 134 | 1960 | Tien Shan | 615 | A-B | |
| Kinzer | 232 | 921 | 1966 | Yu Shan | 826 | A-B | |
| Bull | 693 | 78 | 1966 | Lu Shan | 821 | A-B | |
| Gantner | 60 | 42 | 1966 | Wen Shan | 834 | A-B | |
| Truxton | 282 | 98 | 1966 | Fu Shan | 838 | A-B | |
| Blessman | 69 | 48 | 1967 | Chung Shan | 845 | A-B | |
| Donald W. Wolf | 713 | 129 | 1968 | Hua Shan | 854 | A-B | |
| Register | 233 | 92 | 1966 | Tai Shan | 878 | A-B | |
| Kline | 687 | 120 | 1966 | Shou Shan | 893 | A-B | |
| Raymond W. Herndon | 688 | 121 | 1967 | Chung Nam | | A | |
| George W. Ingram | 62 | 43 | | Kang Shan | | A | |
| **THAILAND** | | | | | | | |
| Hemminger | 746 | | 1959 | Pin Klao | | A-B | |
| **TUNISIA** | | | | | | | |
| Thomas J. Gary | 326 | | 1973 | President Bourguiba | | A-B | |
| **URUGUAY** | | | | | | | |
| Baron | 166 | | 1952 | Uruguay | 1 | A-B | |
| Bronstein | 189 | | 1952 | Artigas | 2 | A-B | |
| **VIET NAM** | | | | | | | |
| Forster | 334 | | 1975 | Trans Khan Du | | A-B | |
| **BRAZIL** | | | | | | | |
| McAnn | 179 | — | 1944 | Bracui | | | Museum Ship Rio de Janiero |
| **UNITED STATES** | | | | | | | |
| Stewart | 238 | | | Stewart | 238 | | Museum Ship Galveston, Texas |

**Explanation:**
A — Active 1979
B — Active 1986

DESTROYER ESCORTS OF WORLD WAR II.

It is the Rising Sun on the Matsuhi, formerly the ATHERTON (DE-169). It was transferred to the Philippines and is now the Rajah Humabon.

*This aerial view taken from 300' shows the arrangement of this Cannon class Destroyer Escort* ***USS GUSTAFSON DE182****. Fitted with 3" guns and high bridge this is but one of 66 units built during the war. The* ***GUSTAFSON*** *was transferred to the Dutch Navy in 1950.* *USN*

## CANNON Class

### DE112-113, 162-197, 739-750, 763-771

### GENERAL INFORMATION

| | |
|---|---|
| Length Overall | 308'-0" |
| Length at Waterline | 300'-0" |
| Beam | 36'-10" |
| Shaft Horsepower | 6,000 |
| Trail Speed | 20.2 Knots |
| War Endurance | 10,800 Miles/12 Knots |
| Displacement | 1,525 Tons |
| Complement | 15 Officers 201 Men |
| Fuel Capacity | 316 Tons |

### ARMAMENT

3-3"/50 cal guns-Main Battery
1-40mm Twin gun
1-Triple Torpedo Tube
8-20mm guns
1-Hedgehog
2-Depth Charge Tracks
8-"K" gun projectors

A total of 72 ships of this class were built with 66 being commissioned into the US Navy. The other 6 (DE106-111) were built for Lend-Lease for France. The external appearance was similar to the **BUCKLEYS.** However, this class has the reduced horsepower due to its Diesel-Electric-Drive. This class was also known as the "DET" class.

The first ship of this class was the USS LEVY DE162, commissioned at Federal Shipbuilding Co., Newark, NJ, on May 13, 1943. The First Commanding Officer was CDR F.W. Schmidt. Originally, this class was to have 252 units built, but with the program cuts of 1943 and 44, this class, like others, only had a portion of the ships actually built. Like other Destroyer Escorts, improved anti-aircraft batteries were installed with the removal of the amidships torpedo tubes.

Like the EVARTS class, the Navy considered this class unsatisfactory. But rather than wholesale scrapping, these ships were put on the sale block. Six ships served with Navy Reserve and by 1950 only 3 ships remained on the Navy list. During the 1940's, 50's and 60's many ships were sold to Foreign Navies and as of 1986 some ships are still active units.

*With a passenger on the "high-line" the **USS HEMMINGER DE746** is shown here in 1944. Retaining her original configuration with safety stop guards around her guns to prevent the ship's gunners firing into their own ship during the heat of battle.* *80G375213*

CANNON (DET) CLASS

| | | | | | |
|---|---|---|---|---|---|
| DE99 | CANNON | Dravo | 26/ 9/43 | 19/12/44 | Brazil 12/44 Scrapped 73 |
| DE100 | CHRISTOPHER | " | 23/10/43 | 19/12/44 | Brazil 12/44 |
| DE101 | ALGER | " | 12/11/43 | 10/ 3/45 | Brazil 3/45 Scrapped 64 |
| DE102 | THOMAS | " | 21/11/43 | 13/ 3/47 | China 10/48 |
| DE103 | BOSTWICK | " | 1/12/43 | 30/ 4/46 | China 12/48 |
| DE104 | BREEMAN | " | 12/12/43 | 26/ 4/46 | China 10/48 |
| DE105 | BURROWS | " | 19/12/43 | 14/ 6/46 | Holland 6/50 Sold 2/68 |
| DE112 | CARTER | " | 3/ 5/44 | 10/ 4/46 | China 12/48 Scrapped 11/72 |

*Enroute to the invasion of Iwo Jima with her charge, the **USS RIDDLE DE185** is shown here transferring official mail to the **USS ELDORADO AGC 11.** Note the light color on the stack of the **RIDDLE**.* *80G375213*

| | | | | | |
|---|---|---|---|---|---|
| DE113 | C.L.EVANS | " | 25/ 6/44 | 29/ 5/47 | France 3/52 Scrapped |
| DE162 | LEVY | Fedrl | 13/ 5/43 | 4/ 4/47 | |
| DE163 | McCONNELL | " | 28/ 5/43 | 29/ 6/46 | Scrapped 10/72 |
| DE164 | OSTERHAUS | " | 12/ 6/43 | 26/ 6/46 | Scrapped 11/72 |
| DE165 | PARKS | " | 23/ 6/43 | 3/46 | Scrapped 7/72 |
| DE166 | BARON | " | 5/ 7/43 | 26/ 4/46 | Uruguay 5/52 |
| DE167 | ACREE | " | 19/ 7/43 | 1/ 4/46 | Scrapped 7/72 |
| DE168 | AMICK | " | 26/ 7/43 | 16/ 5/47 | Japan 6/55 |
| DE169 | ATHERTON | " | 29/ 8/43 | 10/12/45 | Japan 6/55 |
| DE170 | BOOTH | " | 19/ 9/43 | 4/ 4/46 | Philippines 12/67 |
| DE171 | CARROLL | " | 24/10/43 | 19/ 6/46 | Scrapped 12/66 |
| DE172 | COONER | " | 21/ 8/43 | 25/ 6/46 | Scrapped 7/72 |
| DE173 | ELDRIDGE | " | 27/ 8/43 | 17/ 6/46 | Greece 1/51 |
| DE174 | MARTS | " | 3/ 9/43 | 20/ 3/45 | Brazil 3/45 |
| DE175 | PENNEWILL | " | 15/ 9/43 | 1/ 8/44 | Brazil 8/44 |
| DE176 | MICKA | " | 23/ 9/43 | 12/ 6/46 | Scrapped 5/67 |
| DE177 | REYBOLD | " | 29/ 9/43 | 15/ 8/44 | Brazil 8/44 Scrapped 7/72 |
| DE178 | HERZOG | " | 6/10/43 | 1/ 8/44 | Brazil 8/44 Scrapped 2/66 |
| DE179 | McANN | " | 11/10/43 | 15/ 8/44 | Brazil 8/44 |
| DE180 | TRUMPETER | " | 16/10/43 | 5/12/47 | Target 73 |
| DE181 | STRAUB | " | 25/10/43 | 17/10/47 | Sold 8/73 |
| DE182 | GUSTAFSON | " | 1/11/43 | 26/ 6/46 | Holland 10/50 Sold 2/68 |
| DE183 | S.S.MILES | " | 4/11/43 | 28/ 3/46 | France 8/50 Scrapped 68 |
| DE184 | WESSON | " | 11/11/43 | 25/ 7/46 | Italy 1/51 Scrapped 1/72 |
| DE185 | RIDDLE | " | 17/11/43 | 8/ 6/46 | France 8/50 Scrapped 5/64 |
| DE186 | SWEARER | " | 24/11/43 | 27/ 8/47 | France 8/50 Scrapped 5/64 |
| DE187 | STERN | " | 1/12/43 | 26/ 4/46 | Holland 5/51 Sold 2/68 |
| DE188 | O'NEILL | " | 6/12/43 | 2/ 5/46 | Holland 10/50 Sold 2/68 |
| DE189 | BRONSTEIN | " | 13/12/43 | 5/11/45 | Uruguay 5/52 |
| DE190 | BAKER | " | 23/12/43 | 4/ 5/46 | France 3/52 Sunk 70 |
| DE191 | COFFMAN | " | 27/12/43 | 30/ 4/46 | Sold 73 |
| DE192 | EISNER | " | 1/ 1/43 | 5/ 7/46 | Holland 3/50 Sold 2/68 |
| DE193 | G.THOMAS | " | 24/ 1/44 | 27/ 3/47 | Greece 1/51 |
| DE194 | WINGFIELD | " | 28/ 1/44 | 26/ 8/47 | France 10/50 |
| DE195 | THORNHILL | " | 1/ 2/44 | 17/ 6/47 | Italy 1/51 |
| DE196 | RINEHART | " | 12/ 2/44 | 17/ 7/46 | Holland 6/50 Sold 2/68 |
| DE197 | ROCHE | " | 21/ 2/44 | Mined 22/ 9/45 | Scuttled 3/46 |
| DE739 | BANGUST | WPS | 30/10/43 | 17/11/46 | Peru 2/52 |
| DE740 | WATERMAN | " | 30/11/43 | 31/ 5/46 | Peru 10/49 |
| DE741 | WEAVER | " | 31/12/43 | 3/ 7/47 | Peru 10/49 |
| DE742 | HILBERT | " | 4/ 2/44 | 19/ 6/46 | Sold 10/73 |
| DE743 | LAMONS | " | 29/ 2/44 | 14/ 6/46 | Sold 10/73 |
| DE744 | KYNE | " | 4/ 4/44 | 17/ 6/46 | NRF Sold 11/73 |
| DE745 | SYNDER | " | 5/ 5/44 | 5/ 5/60 | NRF 46-60 Scrapped 8/72 |
| DE746 | HEMMINGER | " | 30/ 5/44 | 17/ 6/46 | NRF 46-50 Thailand 7/59 |
| DE747 | BRIGHT | " | 30/ 6/44 | 19/ 4/46 | France 11/50 Sold 65 |
| DE748 | TILLS | " | 8/ 8/44 | 6/46 | NRF 46-58 Target 4/69 |
| DE749 | ROBERTS | " | 2/ 9/44 | 3/ 3/46 | NRF 46-50 Target 68 |
| DE750 | McCLELLAND | " | 19/ 9/44 | 15/ 5/46 | NRF 47-59 Sold 73 |
| DE763 | CATES | TampSB | 15/12/43 | 28/ 3/47 | France 11/50 Sold 65 |
| DE764 | GANDY | " | 7 2/44 | 17/ 6/46 | Italy 1/51 Scrapped 71 |
| DE765 | E.K.OLSEN | " | 10/ 4/44 | 17/ 6/46 | NRF 46-50 Sold 10/73 |
| DE766 | SLATER | " | 1/ 5/44 | 26/ 9/47 | Greece 3/51 |
| DE767 | OSWALD | " | 12/ 6/44 | 30/ 4/46 | Scrapped 8/72 |
| DE768 | EBERT | " | 12/ 7/44 | 14/ 6/46 | Greece 3/51 |
| DE769 | N.A.SCOTT | " | 31/ 7/44 | 30/ 4/46 | Sold 68 |
| DE770 | MUIR | " | 30/ 8/44 | 9/47 | Korea 2/56 |
| DE771 | SUTTON | " | 12/12/44 | 19/ 3/48 | Korea 2/56 |

*The Japanese Self Defense Force ship* ***HATSUHI FF6*** *is shown here in June 1955. Formerly the* ***USS ATHERTON DE169.*** *This ship again was transferred to the Philippine Navy after being paid off in September 1976.* *HN46123*

# EDSALL CLASS

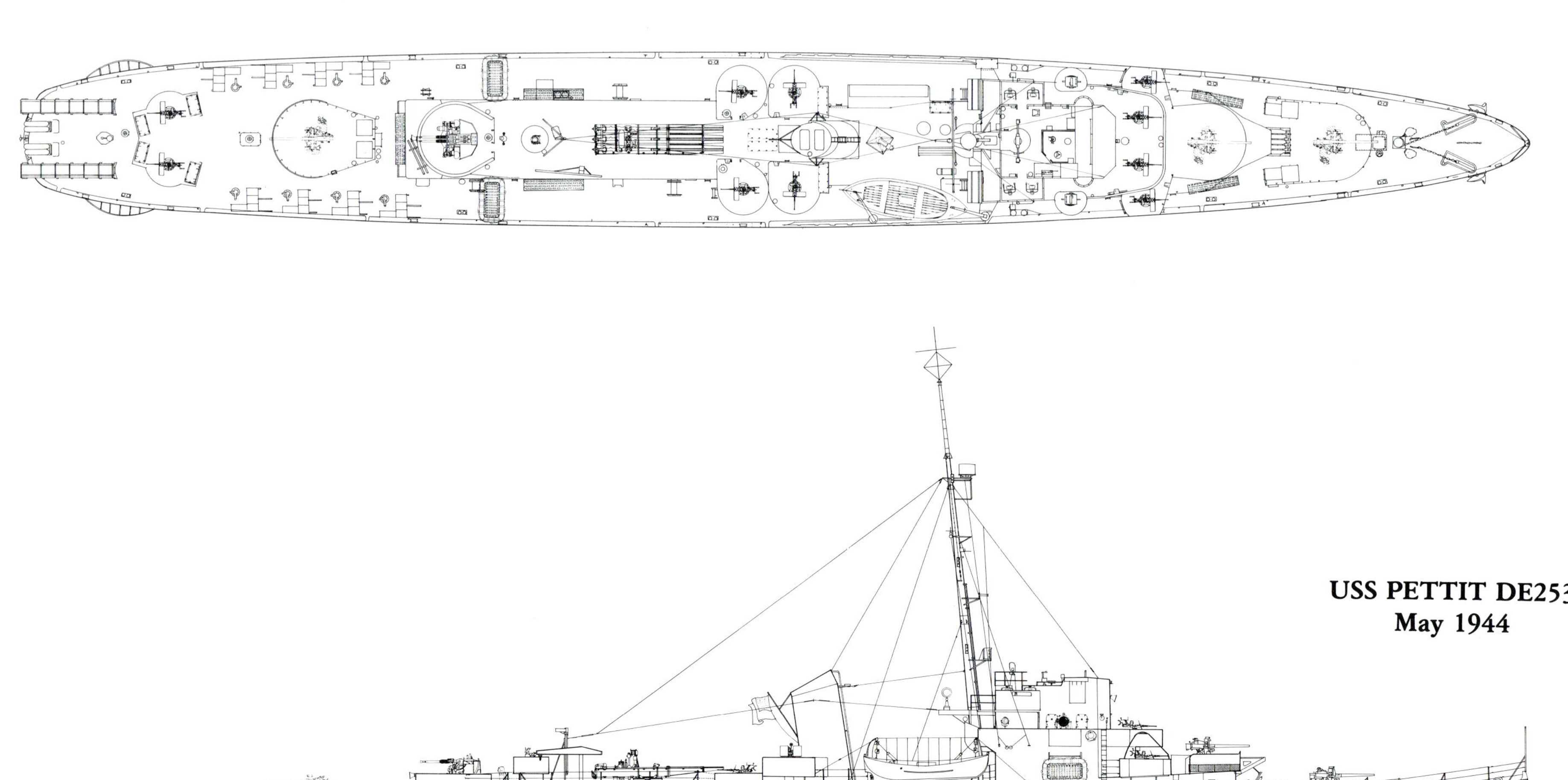

*The **USS BRISTER DE327** is shown off Norfolk Navy Yard in July 1944. Fitted with 40mm guns amidships this EDSALL class is also equipped with HF-DF atop her stub mast.* 19N70334

## EDSALL Class

**DE238-255, 316-338, 382-401**

### GENERAL INFORMATION

| | |
|---|---|
| Length Overall | 306'-0" |
| Length at Waterline | 300'-0" |
| Beam | 36'-10" |
| Shaft Horsepower | 6,000 |
| Trail Speed | 20.9 Knots |
| War Endurance | 5,100 Miles/12 Knots |
| Displacement | 1.490 Tons |
| Complement | 8 Officers 201 Men |
| Fuel Capacity | 312 Tons |

### ARMAMENT

3-3"/50 cal guns-Main Battery
1-Twin 40mm gun
8-20mm guns
1-Triple Torpedo Tube
1-Hedgehog
2-Depth Charge Tracks
8-"K" gun projector

Similar to the **BUCKLEYS** in external appearance with 3" guns, long hull and high bridge superstructure. A total of 85 ships of this class were built by two shipyards, Consolidated Steel Co., of Orange, Texas and Brown Shipbuilding of Houston, Texas. The first Destroyer Escort of this class to be built and commissioned was the USS Edsall De129. It was commissioned on April 10, 1943 at Orange, Texas, with LCDR E.C. Woodward, commanding. These ships were powered by Fairbanks-Morse Diesel engines (FMR).

This class, like the **BUCKLEYS,** were scheduled to have there 3" guns replaced by the better 5"/38, however, these plans were cancelled. The **USS CAMP DE251** was the only ship of this class to get the 5" guns. This was due to an early 1945 collision the ship had and repairs were made that called for the change. Probably the most famous ship of this class was the **USS PILLSBURY DE133,** which took part in the capture of the German submarine U-505 in the Atlantic in 1944.

The US Coast Guard manned 30 Destroyer Escorts during the war and all were of the **EDSALL** class. The only ship of the Coast Guard staffed ships lost during the war was the **USS LEOPOLD DE319,** which was torpedoed by a German U-Boat off Iceland on 9 March 1944. Only 28 men survived from the crew. After the war all Coast Guard Destroyer Escorts were decommissioned, but during the Korean War 12 **EDSALLS** were recommissioned as Coast Guard Ocean Station Ships.

Like other classes of Destroyer Escorts during the war, the Triple Torpedo Tubes were replaced by more anti-aircraft guns. During the invasion on Anzio, early in 1944, several escorts mounted Army single 40mm guns amidships in place of the Torpedoes. These later were removed and replaced with power driven 40mm Twin guns, which were director controlled. Also, stern mounted 20mm guns were added for more firepower.

After the end of the war, the remaining 81 "FMR's" were decommissioned and put into reserves. But in 1950, 4 of these ships were put back into service for the Korean War. In 1954, the 12 Coast Guard **EDSALL's** were returned to the US Navy and several were converted into DER's (Destroyer Escort Radar Picket Ships). By 1960, only two of these ships served as active units of the Fleet and these were soon decommissioned. Three were used as Naval Reserve training ships in the 60's and the **USS BARBER DE161** was transferred to Mexico in 1973.

EDSALL (FMR) CLASS

| | | | | | |
|---|---|---|---|---|---|
| DE129 | EDSALL | Cons | 10/ 4/43 | 11/ 6/46 | Sold 6/68 |
| DE130 | JACOB JONES | " | 29/ 4/43 | 26/ 7/46 | Sold 1/71 |
| DE131 | HAMMANN | " | 17/ 5/43 | 25/10/45 | Sold 10/72 |
| DE132 | R.E.PEARY | " | 31/ 5/43 | 13/ 6/43 | Sold 9/67 |
| DE133 | PILLSBURY | " | 7/ 6/43 | 20/ 6/60 | DER Sold 7/65 |
| DE134 | POPE | " | 25/ 6/43 | 17/ 5/46 | Sold 1/71 |
| DE135 | FLAHERTY | " | 26/ 6/43 | 17/ 6/46 | Sold 11/66 |
| DE136 | F.C.DAVIS | " | 14/ 7/43 | | Torpedoed sunk 24/4/45 |
| DE137 | H.C.JONES | " | 21/ 7/43 | 2/ 5/47 | Sold 7/72 |
| DE138 | D.L.HOWARD | " | 29/ 7/43 | 17/ 6/46 | Sold 10/72 |
| DE139 | FARQUHAR | " | 5/ 8/43 | 14/ 6/46 | Sold 10/72 |
| DE140 | J.R.Y.BLAKELY | " | 16/ 8/43 | 14/ 6/46 | Sold 1/71 |
| DE141 | HILL | " | 16/ 8/43 | 7/ 6/46 | Sold 10/72 |
| DE142 | FESSENDEN | " | 25/ 8/43 | 30/ 6/60 | DER142(10/51) Target 12/67 |
| DE143 | FISKE | " | 25/ 8/43 | | Torpedoed sunk 2/8/44 |
| DE144 | FROST | " | 30/ 8/43 | 18/ 6/46 | Sold 12/66 |

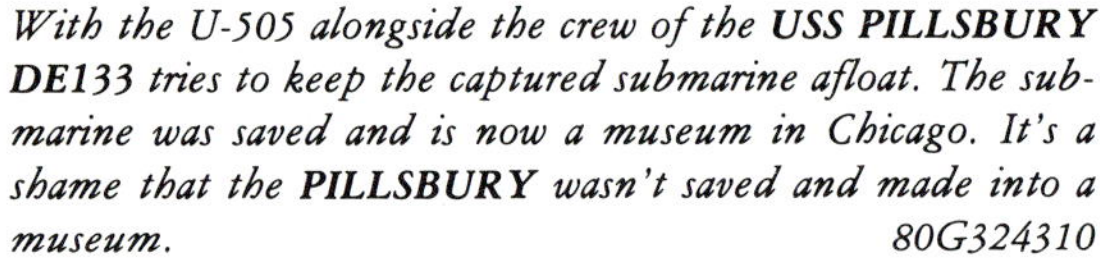

*With the U-505 alongside the crew of the **USS PILLSBURY DE133** tries to keep the captured submarine afloat. The submarine was saved and is now a museum in Chicago. It's a shame that the **PILLSBURY** wasn't saved and made into a museum.* *80G324310*

| | | | | | |
|---|---|---|---|---|---|
| DE145 | HUSE | ” | 30/ 8/43 | 6/65 | NRF Sold 6/74 |
| DE146 | INCH | ” | 8/ 9/43 | 17/ 5/46 | Sold 10/72 |
| DE147 | BLAIR | ” | 13/ 9/43 | 28/ 6/46 | DER147(12/57) Sold 12/72 |
| DE148 | BROUGH | ” | 18/ 9/43 | 22/ 3/46 | Sold 10/66 |
| DE149 | CHATELAIN | ” | 22/ 9/43 | 14/ 6/46 | Sold 8/73 |
| DE150 | NEUNZER | ” | 27/ 9/43 | 1/47 | Sold 7/72 |
| DE151 | POOLE | ” | 29/ 9/43 | 1/47 | Sold 1/71 |
| DE152 | PETERSON | ” | 29/ 9/43 | | ASW Sold 8/73 |
| DE238 | STEWART | Brown | 31/ 5/43 | 27/ 3/46 | Memorial Galveston, TX |
| DE239 | STURTEVANT | ” | 16/ 6/43 | 31/10/56 | DER(10/56) Scrapped 9/73 |
| DE240 | MOORE | ” | 1/ 7/43 | 30/ 6/47 | Target 4/74 |
| DE241 | KEITH | ” | 19/ 7/43 | 20/ 7/46 | Scrapped 11/72 |
| DE242 | TOMICH | ” | 27/ 7/43 | 20/ 9/46 | Scrapped 11/72 |
| DE243 | J.R.WARD | ” | 5/ 7/43 | 13/ 6/46 | Sold 1/71 |
| DE244 | OTTERSTETTER | ” | 6/ 8/43 | 20/ 6/60 | Target 8/74 |
| DE245 | SLOAT | ” | 16/ 8/43 | 6/ 8/47 | Sold 1/71 |
| DE246 | SNOWDEN | ” | 23/ 8/43 | 6/ 8/47 | Sold 1/71 |
| DE247 | STANTON | ” | 7/ 8/43 | 2/ 6/47 | Sold 12/70 |
| DE248 | SWASEY | ” | 31/ 8/43 | 15/ 3/46 | Scrapped 11/72 |
| DE249 | MARCHAND | ” | 8/ 9/43 | 25/ 4/47 | Scrapped 1/71 |
| DE250 | HURST | ” | 30/ 8/43 | 1/ 5/46 | MEXICO 10/73 |
| DE251 | CAMP | ” | 16/ 9/43 | 13/ 2/51 | DER(12/55) Vietnam |
| De252 | H.D.CROW | ” | 27/ 9/43 | 22/ 5/46 | Scrapped 9/68 |
| DE253 | PETTIT | ” | 23/ 9/43 | 6/ 5/46 | Target 9/74 |
| DE254 | RICKETTS | ” | 5/10/43 | 17/ 4/46 | Scrapped 11/72 |
| DE255 | SELLSTROM | ” | 12/10/43 | 6/60 | DER(10/56) Scrapped 4/67 |
| DE316 | HARVESON | Cons | 12/10/43 | 30/ 6/60 | DER(2/51) Scrapped 12/66 |
| DE317 | JOYCE | ” | 30/ 9/43 | 17/ 6/60 | DER(10/51) Scrapped 12/72 |
| DE318 | KIRKPATRICK | ” | 23/10/43 | 24/ 6/60 | DER(10/51) Scrapped 8/74 |
| DE319 | LEOPOLD | ” | 18/10/43 | | Torpedoed 10/4/44 |
| DE320 | MENGES | ” | 26/10/43 | 1/47 | Scrapped 1/71 |
| DE321 | MOSLEY | ” | 30/10/43 | 15/ 3/46 | Scrapped 1/71 |
| DE322 | NEWELL | ” | 30/10/43 | 21/ 9/68 | CG(7/51) Scrapped 12/71 |
| DE323 | PRIDE | ” | 13/11/43 | 26/ 4/46 | CG(7/51) Scrapped 1/71 |
| DE324 | FALGOUT | ” | 15/11/43 | 18/ 4/47 | CG(8/51) Target 6/75 |
| DE325 | LOWE | ” | 22/11/43 | 20/ 9/68 | CG(7/51) Scrapped 9/68 |
| DE326 | T.J.GARY | ” | 27/11/43 | 22/10/73 | DER Tunisia 10/73 |
| DE327 | BRISTER | ” | 30/11/43 | 4/10/46 | DER Taiwan 11/71 |
| DE328 | FINCH | ” | 13/12/43 | 4/10/46 | CG(8/51) Scrapped 2/74 |
| DE329 | KRETCHMER | ” | 12/13/43 | 1/10/73 | CG(6/51) Scrapped 5/74 |
| DE330 | O'REILLY | ” | 28/12/43 | 15/ 6/46 | Scrapped 4/72 |
| DE331 | KOINER | ” | 27/12/43 | 68 | CG(6/51) Scrapped 9/69 |
| DE332 | PRICE | ” | 12/ 1/44 | 30/ 6/60 | DER |
| DE333 | STRICKLAND | ” | 10/ 1/44 | 15/ 6/46 | DER Scrapped 10/72 |

*This Coast Guard-manned Destroyer Escort was torpedoed in the stern two weeks after this photograph was taken of the* ***USS MENGES DE320.*** *Fitted with the stern of the bow-torpedoed* ***USS HOLDER DE404,*** *the* ***MENGES*** *served again.* *USCG*

*The **USS COCKRILL DE398** off New Jersey in February 1945 is seen from this 300' aerial view. Fitted with additional 40mm guns amidships and HF-DF antenna.* 19N78350

*A stern quarter view of the **USS J. RICHARD WARD DE242** shows off her depth charge battery in this May 1944 photograph. At anchor off New York she is painted in measure 22 camouflage.* 19N70848

| | | | | | |
|---|---|---|---|---|---|
| DE334 | FORSTER | ,, | 25/ 1/44 | 15/ 6/46 | CG(6/51) Vietnam 9/71 |
| DE335 | DANIEL | ,, | 24/ 1/44 | 12/ 4/46 | Scrapped 1/71 |
| DE336 | R.O.HALE | ,, | 3/ 2/44 | 15/ 7/63 | DER Scrapped 8/74 |
| DE337 | D.W.PETERSON | ,, | 17/ 2/44 | 27/ 3/46 | Scrapped 1/71 |
| DE338 | M.H.RAY | ,, | 28/ 2/44 | 3/46 | Scrapped 3/67 |
| DE382 | RAMSDEN | ,, | 19/10/43 | 23/ 6/60 | CG(6/54) Target ? |
| DE383 | MILLS | ,, | 12/10/43 | 27/10/70 | DER NRF |
| DE384 | RHODES | ,, | 25/10/43 | 10/ 7/63 | DER Scrapped |
| DE385 | RICHEY | ,, | 30/10/43 | 1/47 | CG(6/54) Target 7/69 |
| DE386 | SAVAGE | ,, | 29/10/43 | 17/10/69 | DER |
| DE387 | VANCE | ,, | 1/11/43 | 10/10/69 | CG(5/51) DER |
| DE388 | LANSING | ,, | 10/11/43 | 21/ 5/65 | DER Scrapped 2/74 |
| DE389 | DURANT | ,, | 16/11/43 | 27/ 2/46 | CG(5/51) Scrapped 4/74 |
| DE390 | CALCATERRA | ,, | 17/11/43 | 2/ 7/73 | DER sold 5/74 |
| DE391 | CHAMBERS | ,, | 22/11/43 | 20/ 6/60 | DER sold 74 |
| DE392 | MERRILL | ,, | 27/11/43 | 12/ 9/47 | Sold 74 |
| DE393 | HAVERFIELD | ,, | 29/11/43 | 30/ 6/71 | DER sold 12/71 |
| DE394 | SWENNING | ,, | 1/12/43 | 25/ 9/47 | Scrapped 7/72 |
| DE395 | WILLIS | ,, | 10/12/43 | 12/ 9/47 | Scrapped 7/72 |
| DE396 | JANSSEN | ,, | 18/12/43 | 12/ 4/46 | Scrapped 7/72 |
| DE397 | WILHOITE | ,, | 16/12/43 | 2/ 7/69 | DER Scrapped 7/72 |
| DE398 | COCKRILL | ,, | 24/12/43 | 21/ 6/46 | Target 73 |
| DE399 | STOCKDALE | ,, | 31/12/43 | 18/ 4/47 | Target 72 |
| DE400 | HISSEM | ,, | 13/ 1/44 | 15/ 5/70 | DER Target 75 |
| DE401 | HOLDER | ,, | 18/ 1/44 | | Torpedoed 11/4/44 |

*One of the few postwar escorts to be converted to a radar picket ship the* **USS HISSEM DE400** *is shown here in November 1960. Many changes are obvious for this EDSALL class escort from her World War Two configuration.* USN1052910

*Needing a fresh coat of paint the dazzled camouflaged* **USS POPE DE134** *is shown here at sea in 1944.* 80G383897

*Painted in overall Navy Blue paint the* **USS BRISTER DE327** *is laying dead in the water in this late war photograph. Outfitted with a quad 40mm gun aft and two 40mm twin guns amidships. This was the ultimate anti-aircraft arrangement of the war time EDSALL'S.* USN

# JOHN C. BUTLER CLASS

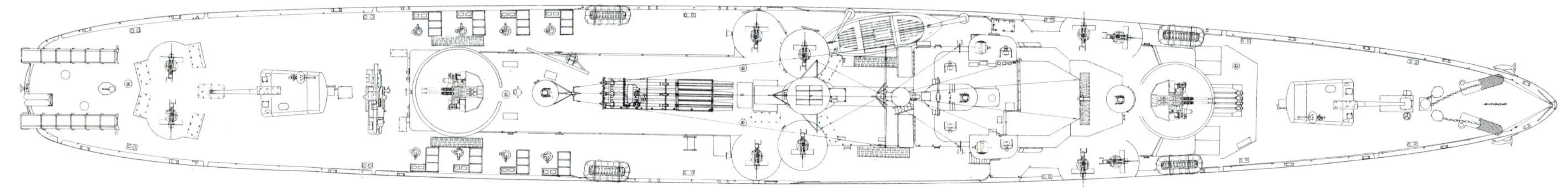

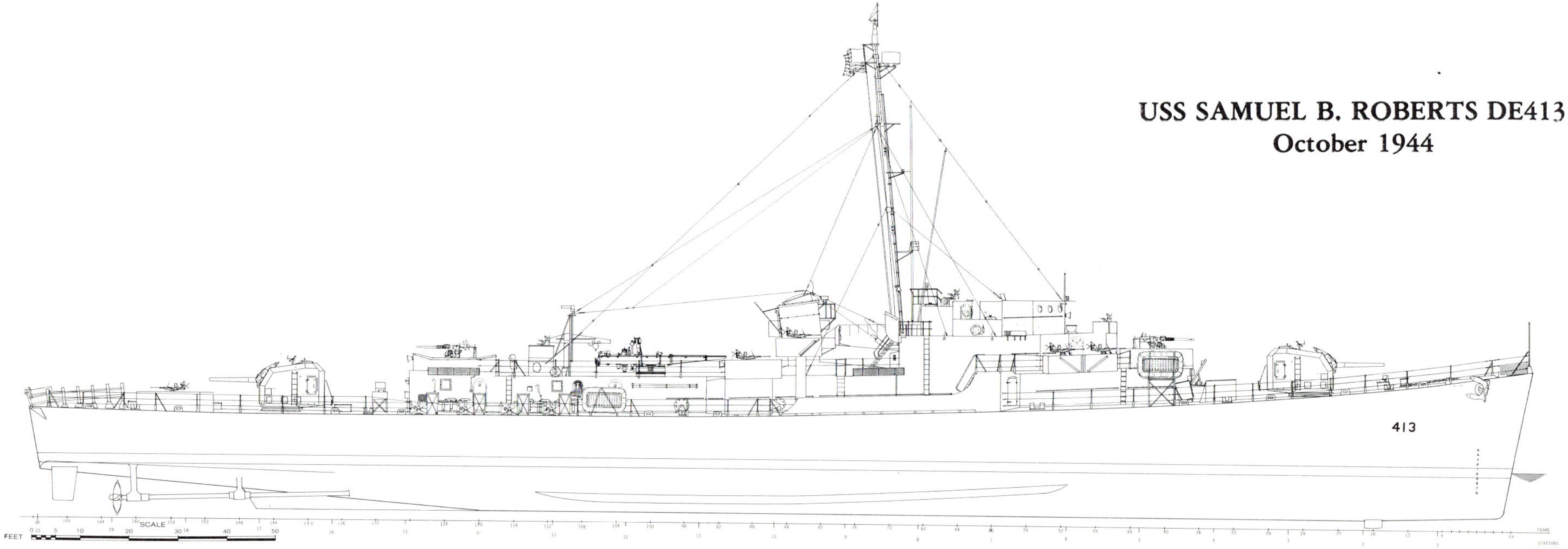

**USS SAMUEL B. ROBERTS DE413**
**October 1944**

*Wearing the uncommon measure 12 camouflage for a Destroyer Escort the* ***USS DOYLE C. BARNES DE353*** *is seen off Boston in September 1944. This ship was built in Orange, Texas. USN*

## JOHN C. BUTLER Class

### DE39-372, 402-424, 438-450, 508-510, 531-540

### GENERAL INFORMATION

| | |
|---|---|
| Length Overall | 306'-0" |
| Length at Waterline | 300'-0" |
| Beam | 36'-10" |
| Shaft Horsepower | 12,000 |
| Trail Speed | 24.15 Knots |
| War Endurance | 4,650 Miles/12 Knots |
| Displacement | 1,600 Tons |
| Complement | 14 Officers 201 Men |
| Fuel Capacity | 347 Tons |

### ARMAMENT

2-5"/38 cal guns-Main Battery
2-Twin 40mm guns
1-Triple Torpedo Tube
10-20mm guns
1 Hedgehog
2-Depth Charge Tracks
8-"K" gun projector

A total of 283 ships of this class were to be built, however, only 83 were completed during the war. Two ships, **USS WAGNER DE539** and **USS VANDIVER DE540,** were completed in the 50's. They were similar to the **RUDDERROW** class in exterior appearance with 5" guns and low bridge superstructure. The first ship of the class built and commissioned was the **USS EDWARD H. ALLEN DE531.** It was built by Boston Navy Shipyard and commissioned on December 16, 1943 with LCDR M.M. Sanford commanding. The ships were also known as the "WGT" class due to the Westinghouse-Geared Turbines.

Several different armament arrangements were installed on this class of Destroyer Escort as built. Early completed units were built with two 40mm twin guns plus the 20mm guns for the anti-aircraft battery. Six ships were built with one quad 40mm gun aft and one twin 40mm gun forward and two twin 40mm guns amidships in place of the Torpedo Tubes. Two ships were built with the quad 40mm gun aft, a twin 40mm gun forward and no torpedo tubes or additional guns added.

At the end of the war 79 "WGT's" were on the Navy's list, with 4 ships lost during the war. The most famous ship of this class was the **USS SAMUEL B. ROBERTS DE 413,** which was lost during the battle off Samar in October 1944. Only six ships were kept active with the fleet after the war, with the rest being placed in reserves. During the Korean War 32 Destroyer Escorts of this class were re-commissioned. By 1960, only 11 ships were left in service and all of these being reserve training fleet. Two ships (DE440 and 509) were transferred to the Portuguese Navy in the late 1950's.

JOHN C. BUTLER (WGT) CLASS

| | | | | | |
|---|---|---|---|---|---|
| DE339 | J.C.BUTLER | Cons | 31/ 3/44 | 18/12/57 | Target 6/70 |
| DE340 | O'FLAHERTY | " | 8/ 4/44 | 1/47 | Scrapped 12/72 |
| DE341 | RAYMOND | " | 15/ 4/44 | 22/ 9/58 | NRF Scrapped 7/2 |
| DE342 | R.W.SUESENS | " | 26/ 4/44 | 15/ 1/47 | Scrapped 3/72 |
| DE343 | ABERCROMBIE | " | 1/ 5/44 | 15/ 6/46 | Target 1/68 |
| DE344 | OBERRENDER | " | 11/ 5/44 | 11/ 7/45 | Damaged 9/5/45 Target 11/45 |
| DE345 | R.BRAZIER | " | 18/ 5/44 | 16/ 9/46 | Target 1/69 |
| DE346 | E.A.HOWARD | " | 25/ 5/44 | 25/ 9/46 | Scrapped 73 |
| DE347 | J. RUTHERFORD | " | 31/ 5/44 | 21/ 6/46 | Target 12/68 |
| DE348 | KEY | " | 5/ 6/44 | 9/ 7/46 | Scrapped 3/72 |
| DE349 | GENTRY | " | 14/ 6/44 | 2/ 7/46 | Scrapped 1/72 |
| DE350 | TRAW | " | 20/ 6/44 | 7/ 6/46 | Target 8/68 |
| DE351 | M.J.MANUEL | " | 30/ 6/44 | 30/10/57 | Target 8/68 |
| DE352 | NAIFEH | " | 4/ 7/44 | 17/ 6/60 | NRF Target 7/66 |
| DE353 | D.C.BARNES | " | 13/ 7/44 | 15/ 1/47 | Scrapped 9/73 |
| DE354 | K.M.WILLETT | " | 19/ 7/44 | 26/ 2/59 | NRF Target 3/74 |
| DE355 | JACCARD | " | 26/ 7/44 | 30/ 9/46 | Target 10/68 |
| DE356 | L.E.ACREE | " | 1/ 8/44 | 10/10/46 | Sold 6/73 |
| De357 | G.E.DAVIS | " | 11/ 8/44 | 11/11/54 | NRF51-54 Sold 1/74 |
| DE358 | MACK | " | 16/ 8/44 | 11/12/46 | Sold 6/73 |
| DE359 | WOODSON | " | 24/ 8/44 | 11/ 8/62 | NRF 57-62 Sold 8/66 |
| DE360 | J.HUTCHINS | " | 28/ 8/44 | 25/ 2/58 | NRF 46-58 Sold 2/74 |
| DE361 | WALTON | " | 4/ 9/44 | 31/ 5/46 | Target 8/69 |
| DE362 | ROLF | " | 7/ 9/44 | 3/ 6/46 | Sold 9/73 |
| DE363 | PRATT | " | 18/ 9/44 | 14/ 5/46 | Scrapped 1/73 |

*With an escort carrier in the background the* ***USS HOWARD F. CLARK DE533*** *waits to come alongside another ship. This photograph is undated but must have been taken during 1944 or early 1945 due to the type of camouflage painted on her.* USN301278

*From 300' up the* ***USS KENDALL C. CAMPBELL DE443*** *makes turns for high speed in this August 1944 view taken off New York.* USN

| | | | | | |
|---|---|---|---|---|---|
| DE364 | ROMBACH | " | 20/ 9/44 | 9/ 1/58 | NRF 46-58 Sold 12/72 |
| DE365 | McGINTY | " | 25/ 9/44 | 19/ 9/59 | NRF 59-61 Sold 10/69 |
| DE366 | A.C.COCKRELL | " | 7/10/44 | 2/ 7/46 | Target 9/69 |
| DE367 | FRENCH | " | 9/10/44 | 29/ 5/46 | Sold 9/73 |
| DE368 | C.J.DOYLE | " | 16/10/44 | 2/ 7/46 | Target 68 |
| DE369 | T.PARKER | " | 25/10/44 | 1/ 9/67 | NRF Sold 7/68 |
| DE370 | J.L.WILLIAMSON | " | 31/10/44 | 14/ 6/46 | Sold 70 |
| DE371 | PRESLEY | " | 7/11/44 | 20/ 6/46 | Sold 68 |
| DE372 | WILLIAMS | " | 11/11/44 | 4/ 6/46 | Target 6/68 |
| DE402 | R.S.BULL | " | 26/ 2/44 | 3/46 | Target 6/69 |
| DE403 | R.M.ROWELL | " | 9/ 3/44 | 2/ 7/46 | Sold 68 |
| DE404 | EVERSOLE | " | 21/ 3/44 | | Torpedoed 28/10/44 |
| DE405 | DENNIS | " | 20/ 3/44 | 31/ 5/46 | Sold 73 |
| DE406 | EDMONDS | " | 3/ 4/44 | 31/ 5/46 | Scrapped 15/5/72 |
| DE407 | SHELTON | " | 4/ 4/44 | | Torpedoed 3/10/44 |
| DE408 | STRAUS | " | 6/ 4/44 | 15/ 1/47 | Target 67 |
| DE409 | LA PRADE | " | 20/ 4/44 | 11/ 5/46 | Scrapped 1/72 |
| DE410 | JACK MILLER | " | 13/ 4/44 | 1/ 6/46 | Sold 6/68 |
| DE411 | STAFFORD | " | 19/ 4/44 | 16/ 5/46 | Scrapped 3/72 |
| DE412 | W.C.WANN | " | 2/ 5/44 | 31/ 5/46 | Sold 6/68 |
| DE413 | S.B.ROBERTS | " | 28/ 4/44 | | Sunk 25/10/44 |
| DE414 | LE RAY WILSON | " | 10/ 5/44 | 30/ 1/59 | Scrapped 5/72 |
| DE415 | L.C.TAYLOR | " | 13/ 5/44 | 23/ 4/46 | Sold 73 |
| DE416 | M.R.NAWMAN | " | 16/ 5/44 | 30/ 8/60 | NRF Scrapped 7/72 |
| DE417 | O.MITCHELL | " | 14/ 6/44 | 24/ 4/46 | Scrapped 3/72 |
| DE418 | TABBERER | " | 23/ 5/44 | 5/60 | NRF Scrapped 7/72 |
| DE419 | R.F.KELLER | " | 17/ 6/44 | 21/ 9/59 | NRF Sold 73 |
| DE420 | L.E.THOMAS | " | 19/ 6/44 | 3/ 5/46 | Sold 9/73 |
| DE421 | C.T.O'BRIEN | " | 3/ 7/44 | 21/ 2/59 | NRF Sold 3/74 |
| DE422 | D.A.MUNRO | " | 11/ 7/44 | 24/ 6/60 | Target |
| DE423 | DUFILHO | " | 21/ 7/44 | 14/ 5/46 | Sold 73 |
| DE424 | HAAS | " | 2/ 8/44 | 31/ 5/46 | Sold 12/73 |
| DE438 | CORBESIER | Fedrl | 31/ 3/44 | 2/ 7/46 | Sold 12/73 |
| DE439 | CONKLIN | " | 21/ 4/44 | 17/ 1/46 | Sold 5/72 |
| DE440 | McCOY REYNOLDS | " | 2/ 5/44 | 7/ 2/57 | Portugal Scrapped 68 |

*With the war over these Destroyer Escorts are enjoying some peace time upkeep. Here an unknown BUTLER class shows off her newly installed equipment in this November 1945 Mare Island photograph.* 19N91497

*Off Viegues Island in the Caribbean in May 1952 the* ***USS THADDEUS PARKER DE369*** *is little changed from her World War Two configuration. The only change seen in this view is the removal of the torpedo tubes.* USN446907

| | | | | | |
|---|---|---|---|---|---|
| DE441 | W.SEIVERLING | ” | 1/ 6/44 | 21/ 3/47 | Scrapped 9/73 |
| DE442 | U.M.MOORE | ” | 18/ 7/44 | 22/ 5/46 | Target 7/66 |
| DE443 | K.C.CAMPBELL | ” | 31/ 7/44 | 31/ 5/46 | Sold 11/73 |
| DE444 | GOSS | ” | 26/ 8/44 | 15/ 6/44 | NRF 3/72 |
| DE445 | GRADY | ” | 11/ 9/44 | 18/12/57 | NRF 6/69 |
| DE446 | C.E.BRANNON | ” | 1/11/44 | 18/ 6/60 | NRF Sold 10/69 |
| DE447 | A.T.HARRIS | ” | 29/11/44 | 26/ 7/46 | NRF Target 4/69 |
| DE448 | CROSS | ” | 8/ 1/45 | 2/ 1/58 | NRF Sold 3/68 |
| DE449 | HANNA | ” | 27/ 1/45 | 11/12/59 | NRF Sold 12/73 |
| DE450 | J.E.CONNOLLY | ” | 28/ 2/45 | 20/ 6/46 | Target 2/72 |
| DE508 | GILLIGAN | ” | 12/ 5/44 | 31/ 3/59 | NRF Scrapped 3/72 |
| DE509 | FORMORE | ” | 5/10/44 | 7/ 2/57 | Portugal 5/46 |
| DE510 | HEYLIGER | ” | 24/ 3/45 | 20/ 6/46 | Target 69 |
| DE531 | E.H.ALLEN | BosNY | 16/12/43 | 9/ 1/58 | Sold 2/74 |
| DE532 | TWEEDY | ” | 12/ 2/44 | 6/69 | NRF Target 5/70 |
| DE533 | H.F.CLARK | ” | 25/ 5/44 | 15/ 7/46 | Sold 9/73 |
| DE534 | SILVERSTEIN | ” | 14/ 7/44 | 30/ 1/59 | Sold 12/73 |
| DE535 | LEWIS | ” | 5/ 9/44 | 27/ 5/60 | Target 3/66 |
| DE536 | BIVEN | ” | 31/10/44 | 15/ 1/47 | Target 7/69 |
| DE537 | RIZZI | ” | 26/ 6/45 | 28/ 2/58 | Scrapped 74 |
| DE538 | OSBERG | ” | 10/12/45 | 9/57 | Scrapped 3/74 |
| DE539 | WAGNER | ” | 22/11/55 | 3/60 | Target 11/74 |
| DE540 | VANDIVIER | ” | 11/10/55 | 6/60 | Target 11/74 |

*With a contrast of black and light gray paint the* **USS O'FLAHERTY DE340** *sails off New England in June 1944. This 22D camouflage design was originally developed for use on fleet destroyers.* *USN*

*The namesake of the class the* **USS JOHN C. BUTLER DE339** *steams out of Boston in May 1944. She is painted in measure 32 design 22D camouflage. Her crew are still at their maneuvering stations.* *USN*

*This series of close-ups show in detail the* **USS EDWARD H. ALLEN DE531.** *Newly built at Federal Ship Yard in Newark, N.J., in the winter of 1943/44. The details of the depth charge loader racks can be seen along with the many bulkhead details. The "K" guns each are loaded with the standard 300 pound TNT depth charge.* USN

# HIGH SPEED TRANSPORT CLASSES

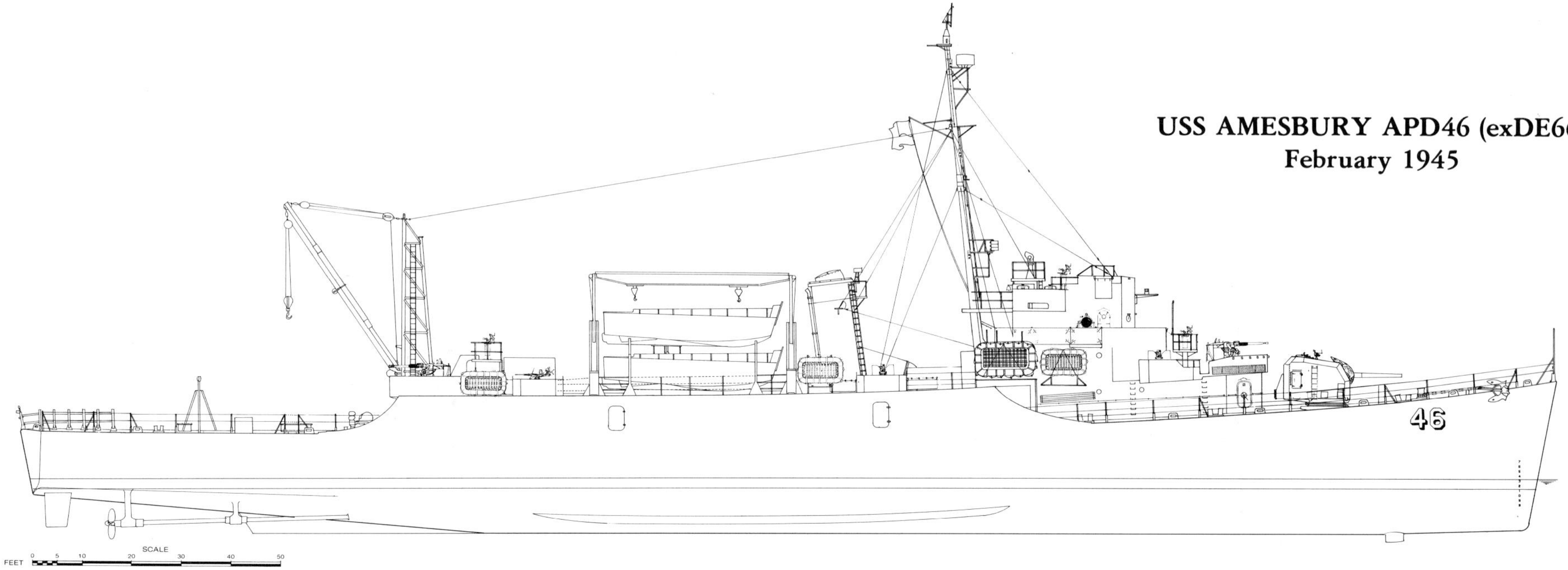

**USS AMESBURY APD46 (exDE66)**
**February 1945**

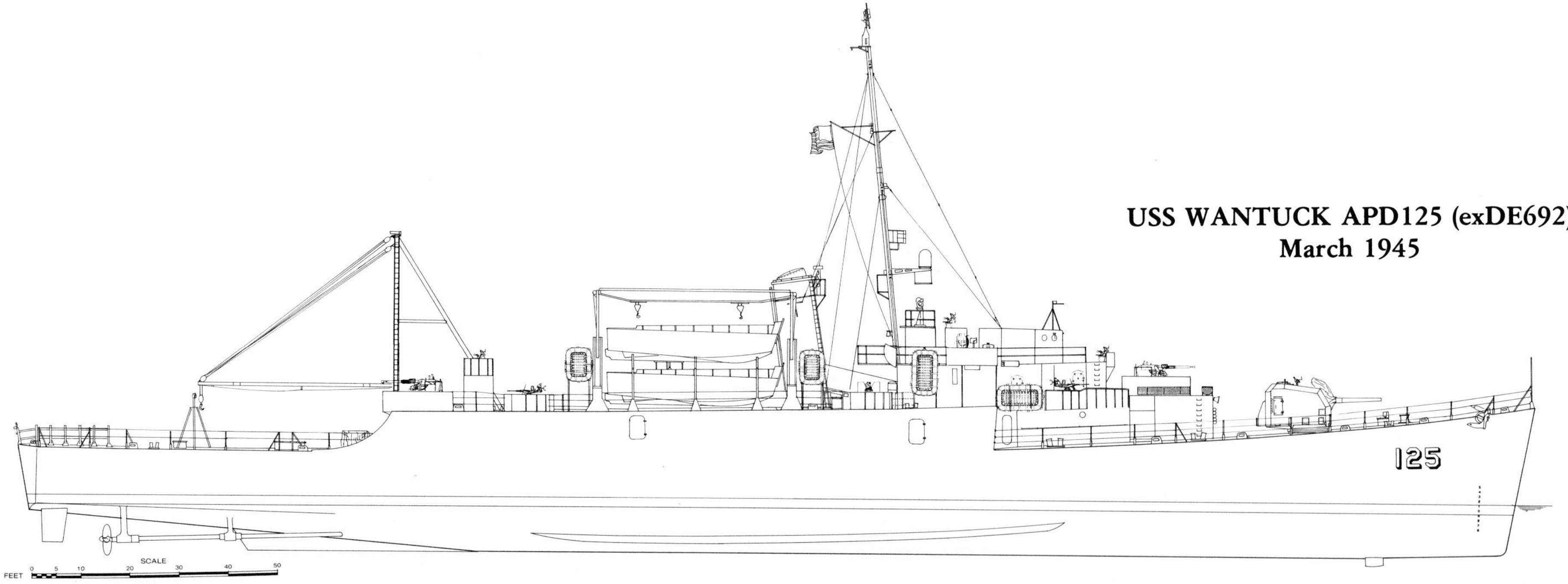

46

SCALE
FEET 0 5 10 20 30 40 50

**USS WANTUCK APD125 (exDE692)**
**March 1945**

125

SCALE
FEET 0 5 10 20 30 40 50

*The ex-Destroyer Escort **USS LLOYD DE209** is seen here as a APD63 off the Philadelphia Navy Yard in September 1944. Painted in green jungle camouflage the **LLOYD** carried 4 LCVP's aft off the stack, and has an enlarged amidships deck house to accommodate the extra troops she carried. Her forward 3" gun has been replaced by a 5" enclosed gun and 40mm twin gun replaces number 2 3" gun.* *19N72335*

## FAST TRANSPORTS (APD's)

In September 1943, the vice CNO suggested the conversion of 100 Destroyer Escorts to APD's and Bombardment ships. In October 1943, plans were drawn up for this conversion. The Bombardment ships were never built, but the APD conversion took place. These ships were designed to carry a lightly equipped Reinforced Battalion, which consisted of 10 Officers and 150 troops. Four 36' LCVP's (landing craft) were installed amidships to carry the troops, supplies, jeeps and trucks that were carried onboard the APD.

The plans called for the conversion of 50 "TE" class ships that were to have there 3" guns replaced with a 5"/38 cal gun forward and 2 twin 40mm guns located aft on the superstructure deck. Boat davits, cradles and an enlarged amidships deck house were installed to house the troops. This conversion was approved by Admiral King on 17 May 1944. The Bureau of Ships (BuShips) also approved the conversion of "TEV's" being built as Destroyer Escorts to APD's.

A total of 95 Destroyer Escorts were converted to APD's and one (APD47), ex DE68) was lost off Okinawa in 1945. Two others were badly damaged and scrapped in 1946. Three ships lasted in service with the Navy until 1969 when they were decommissioned.

*Above: Leaving Mare Island in February 1945 on a sea of glass the* **USS WANTUCK APD125** *was originally DE692. This RUDDEROW type of escort was ideal for the conversion into APD's. Similar to the converted BUCKLEY'S except for the tripod boat boom and the lower bridge.* USN

*Right: With her original high bridge this BUCKLEY class escort can be distinguished between the low bridge RUDDEROW'S. The* **USS BLESSMAN APD48** *was originally DE69 and converted in July 1944. She is seen here in August 1945.* USN

*Painted in standard haze gray paint the* **USS LANING APD55** *is little changed from wartime except for the addition of more antennas on her mast. Built as DE159 the* **LANING** *was converted to an APD in November 1944.* USN

*A forward close-up of the ex-DE206 the* **USS LIDDLE APD60** *is seen at San Francisco in February 1945. She displays three Japanese flags painted on her bridge below an airplane to indicate she shot down three aircraft. A MK51 director has been added behind her forward 40mm twin gun along with other additions.* 19N83401

*With her crew at quarters the* **USS WILLIAM M. HOBBY APD95** *is shown here off South Carolina in April 1945. Originally DE236 the* **HOBBY** *was converted at the Charlestown Navy Yard in February 1944.* 19N81264

*The* ***OLIVER HAZARD PERRY*** *class of frigate is one of the largest classes of US Navy warships to be built since World War Two. The* ***USS MCINERNEY FFG8*** *is seen here in this recent port profile. Fitted with an MK13 Missle launcher, 76mm gun and MK32 torpedo tubes. These vessels have taken over the role that the Destroyer Escorts once had. The ships are 445 feet long with a crew of 200 men.* USN

## POSTWAR DESTROYER ESCORTS

In the post war years, some of the World War Two Destroyer Escorts were used as active Fleet units. New Radar and Sonar were added along with newer types of weapons, mostly to the anti-submarine type. More ships were taken out of the mothball fleet and re-commissioned for the Korean War. Many changes were made to these ships and they would be hard to recognize from their WW2 configuration.

A better Escort was needed to keep up with the newer and faster ships. The first new class of Destroyer Escort to be built after the war were the **USS DEALEY DE1006.** Slightly larger than the WW2 Destroyer Escort, these vessels were commissioned between 1954 and 1957. Proven to be unsuccessful, these ships were scrapped by 1973. The next class was the **USS CLAUD JONES DE1033.** Like the **DEALEY's,** these ships also proved unsuccessful. Built in 1957-58, the ships were sold to Indonesia during 1973-74.

Next came the two units of the **BRONSTEIN** class. Larger than the WW2 Destroyer Escort, these vessels, built during the early 1960's, are still active units of the US Navy. Then came the 10 ships of the **GARCIA DE1040** class, built during the mid-sixties, and the 38 ships of the **KNOX DE1052** class. On June 30 1975, all Escort Ships had there designation changed from "DE" to "FF", thus DE1052 became FF1052. Then came the one of a kind **USS GLOVER AGDE1,** later changed to FF1098. After this came the **USS BROOKE FFG1** class, which were built during 63-66. These ships were essentially the same as the **GARCIA** class.

The **OLIVER HAZARD PERRY FFG7** class is the largest class of escort ships to be built for the US Navy since World War Two. This class, with the **PERRY** being commissioned in 1977, is still being built. About 46 units are now in service and more are on the building blocks.

*Built in 1967 this KNOX class frigate the* ***USS WHIPPLE FF1062*** *is seen here off Hawaii in 1974. Fitted with MK32 torpedos, 5'' guns and missile launcher this 438 foot ship has a crew of 287 men.* USN KN-22730

*Newly built the* ***GEORGE PHILIP FFG12*** *is one of 51 US Navy FFG'S being built. Several of this design have been built for foreign navies. The fully automatic 76mm gun can fire 80 rounds a minute and is director controlled.* USN

*The USS **FISKE DE143** is seen here breaking in two after taking a U-Boat torpedo in the starboard side on 2 August 1944. The ship sank within 10 minutes with the loss of thirty men.* 80G270257

## DESTROYER ESCORTS LOST OR SEVERELY DAMAGED DURING WW2

**USS DONNELL DE56** was on convoy duty 3 May 1944 when she engaged a submarine with depth charges and was simultaneously struck by a torpedo, which blew off her stern. This blast killed 29 men and wounded 25 others. She was towed by **USS REEVES DE156** to Scotland, and used as an accommodation ship by Lisahally, Ireland. She was again towed to Cherbourg, France in August 1944 and supplied electric shore power. In February 1945, the **DONNELL** was taken to England and served as barracks ship at Portland and Plymouth. She was towed back to Philadelphia and in July 1945 was decommissioned and sold for scrap.

**USS FECHTELER DE157** was torpedoed while on convoy duty on 5 May 1944 in the Western Mediterranean. Twenty-nine men were killed and 26 others wounded. The ship broke in two and sank.

**USS SOLAR DE221** was destroyed by an explosion, while at the Naval Ammunition Depot at Earle, NJ on 30 April 1946. This tragedy claimed the lives of 165 men and injured 65 others. The hulk was sunk off New York in May 1946.

**USS UNDERHILL DE686** was struck by a Japanese midget suicide submarine on 24 July 1945. The forward part of the ship was destroyed and survivors gathered on the after section of the ship, which started to sink. These men were picked up by PC804 and the hulk was sunk by gunfire from the Patrol Craft.

**USS RICH DE695** struck a mine while giving assistance to the **USS GLENNON DD 840,** which also struck a mine off the Saint-Marcouf Islands during the Normandy Invasion of France. The stern of the **RICH** was blown off by an explosion and a few minutes later a second went off. The forward section of the ship started to buckle and the ship sank a few minutes later. Of her crew, 27 were killed, 73 wounded and 62 were listed as missing.

**USS ENGLAND DE635** was attacked by Japanese dive bombers on 9 May 1945, and was crashed by one abreast of the bridge on the starboard side. She was towed to Kerama Retto with 37 men killed and 25 wounded. She sailed to Leyte for repairs and on 16 July 1945, she arrived in Philadelphia for conversion to APD. The work on conversion stopped and she was

*Laying in Casablanca Harbor after having her stern blown off, the* ***USS BARR DE576*** *was saved and converted to an APD in July 1944. Torpedoed by a U-Boat on May 29, 1944 in the Atlantic.*
*USN 319603*

decommissioned on 15 October 1945. Then sold for scrap 26 November 1946.

**USS WITTER DE636** was struck by a Japanese aircraft on the starboard side at the waterline. Under her own power, she made Kerama Retto, for temporary repairs. She arrived in Philadelphia for conversion to APD on 16 August 1945. The conversion was cancelled due to the end of the War. The hulk was sold 2 December 1946 for scrapping.

**USS EVERSOLE DE404** was torpedoed by I-45 during the battle of Leyte Gulf on 28 October 1944. The ship was ordered abandoned and while the men were in the water, the submarine surfaced and opened fire, then dived once more. Five minutes later, there was a tremendous underwater explosion, which killed or wounded all the survivors. A total of 139 wounded survivors were picked up by other Destroyer Escorts.

**USS FISKE DE143** was torpedoed on 2 August 1944 by U-804. The torpedo struck the starboard side amidships and within 10 minutes, she broke in two and had to be abandoned. Thirty of her men were killed and 50 badly wounded by the explosion. The survivors were picked up by the **USS FARQUHAR DE139.**

**USS FREDERICK C. DAVIS DE136** was torpedoed on 24 April 1945 by U-546 in the Atlantic. The torpedo struck the port side forward, while she was preparing to attack the submarine. After five minutes, she broke in two and efforts to preserve the buoyancy of the stern failed. Her survivors abandoned the stern and were picked up within three hours by other escorts. The U-546 was also sunk the same day by Destroyer Escorts. The **DAVIS** lost 115 men in her sinking.

**USS HOLDER DE401** was torpedoed by German aircraft on 11 April 1944 in the Mediterranean. She was struck in the port side amidships causing two heavy explosions. Though fires spread and flooding was serious, **HOLDER's** crew remained at their guns to drive off the attackers, without damage to the convoy she was escorting at the time. Alert damage control kept the ship seaworthy and she arrived by tow at Oran for repairs. There it was decided to tow her to New York, were she arrived safely, on 9 June 1944. Decommissioned on 13 September 1944, her forward part of her hull was used to repair the **USS MENGES DE320.** The rest of the hull was sold for scrap in 1947.

*Minutes after hitting a mine which blew off the stern of the* ***USS RICH DE695,*** *she is seen here hitting another mine amidships during the invasion of Normandy. The ship started to buckle and sank in minutes. A large portion of her crew was either killed or missing in this sinking.* NH44312

*Seen before being lost off Okinawa in May 1945 the **USS OBERRENDER DE344** was struck by a kamikaze on the starboard side and was written off as a total loss. She was sunk by US gunfire after the war off Kerama Retto.* USN

**USS LEOPOLD DE319** was torpedoed by U-255 on 9 March 1944. Badly damaged, she was abandoned by her crew and sunk the next day. A total of 28 survivors were picked up by the **USS JOYCE DE171.** The other 171 were lost due to the explosion or drowned.

**USS OBERRENDER DE 344** was struck by a Japanese suicide plane on 9 May 1945 off Okinawa. She was struck on the starboard side, with the aircraft's bomb penetrating the deck and exploding in the forward fireroom. This caused extensive heavy damage and twenty-four sailors were killed or wounded. She was towed to Kerama Retto and was beyond repair. She was decommissioned 11 July 1945 and her hulk was sunk by gunfire on 6 November.

**USS SAMUEL B. ROBERTS DD413** was sunk by Japanese surface ships during the Battle of Samar. While escorting American Escort Carriers on 25 October 1944, she engaged along with other escorts, the Japanese ships in gunfire and torpedoes. She scored a torpedo hit on a cruiser and at least 40 gunfire hits on a second. She was hit by a 14 inch salvo, which opened the port side at number 2 engine room. The ship was abandoned and soon sank. A total of 120 men were picked up after two days in the water.

**USS SHELDON DE407** was attacked by Japanese submarine RO-41, off Seeadler Harbor, Admiralty Island on 3 October 1944. The **SHELDON** was acting as a screen for two escort carriers when struck by a torpedo on the starboard side, which caused severe damage and flooding. The crew was removed by the **USS RICHARD M. ROWELL DE403,** which also took the **SHELDON** under tow. However, she capsized and sank.

*This Coast Guard-manned Destroyer Escort **USS MENGES DE320** is seen shortly after having her stern blown off by a U-Boat torpedo.* USCG-4626